ALL WE LIKE SHEEP

"The authors remind us that Christ followers lack nothing from the Good Shepherd: we are restored, adopted, accepted, protected—we are loved. This book is rich with lessons from ladies who know sheep well; readers discover faith-driven parallels between raising these creatures and walking intimately with God. An insightful, delightful, and inspiring read!"

–Gayle M. Irwin
author of *Walking In Trust* and other inspirational dog books

"I love this book! It flows so smoothly that you do not notice a transition from the real life sheep ranch experience to the relevant scripture verses. The lessons are excellent and will make a great personal or group Bible study. An extra bonus is the glimpse the reader gets about what sheep ranching is really like."

–Susan Bulanda
author of *God's Creatures: A Biblical View of Animals*

"Real-life wisdom and biblical truth! I often felt I was there. I found myself rolling my shoulders, feeling the weight of Jesus skin covering me—making me acceptable to the Father; and, wrinkling my nose trying to smell the stench of Christ's death that would become a fragrant aroma in the Father's nostrils. The parallels drawn were vivid and rich with detail."

–Craig Kirkpatrick
Evangelical Free pastor in Eaton, Colorado

"Full of deep spiritual lessons written with an artful blend of humor and wisdom. True stories are interspersed with questions to encourage application and prayers that lead the reader to the foot of the Cross. For Christians who desire a deeper understanding of the loving way that Jesus leads those who truly desire to hear His voice."

–Norma Gail
Bible teacher, author, devotional writer

"Having worked with sheep all my life, I know how vital it is that sheep have a good shepherd. Just as we shepherd sheep on this earth, Christ shepherds us. Millie and Marilyn have done a wonderful job of taking the experiences they have gained through their sheep management and putting it into words for people to enjoy, learn from, and most importantly gain a new understanding of the relationship between we the sheep and Jesus Christ, our good shepherd."

–Benjamin D. Brown
Doctor of Veterinary Medicine

"Transparent and truthful, engaging and enlightening. The authors, in a sense, use their 'shepherd's crook' to guide the reader into a deeper understanding of the Great Shepherd's love. And they use their 'shepherd's rod' to challenge their readers to grow in faith, learning to enjoy the green meadows and dark valleys. The practical lessons taught are insightful and life changing. The short chapters can be used for personal devotions, or even as a basis for Bible study groups. Marilyn and Millie remind us on each page that sheep are amazing creatures, created by an amazing God."

–Tonya Blessing
author, speaker, co-founder/director Strong Cross Ministries

ALL WE LIKE SHEEP

LESSONS FROM THE SHEEPFOLD

Marilyn Bay Wentz
&
Mildred Nelson Bay

CLADACH
Publishing

All We Like Sheep
Lessons From The Sheepfold

Published by Cladach Publishing
Greeley, Colorado www.cladach.com

Library of Congress Cataloging-in-Publication Data:
Wentz, Marilyn Bay, 1960- author.
All we like sheep : lessons from the sheepfold / Marilyn Bay Wentz and Mildred Nelson Bay.
pages cm
Includes bibliographical references and index.
ISBN 978-0-9891014-3-1 (alk. paper)
1. Farm life—Religious aspects—Christianity. 2. Sheep—Religious aspects—Christianity. I. Bay, Mildred Nelson, 1938- author. II. Title.
S521.W46 2015
636.3--dc23 2015027584

ISBN-10: 0989101436 ISBN-13: 9780989101431

Printed in the United States of America

Table of Contents

Dedicated to Mildred's husband and Marilyn's father,

Marvin Bay

and the other two Bay siblings,

Michelle (Bay) Still *and* Marla (Bay) Suarez

We all shared in the farm work and shepherding from 1968 until the youngest sibling, Marla, left home in 1983. We hope you three like the way we told these sheep-raising stories.

"We are his people, the sheep of his pasture." Ps. 100:3

1
The Shepherd Will Calm Your Fears

I sought the Lord and He heard me and delivered me from all my fears.

–Psalm 34:4 (NKJV)

What a gorgeous summer morning! The sun shone brilliantly, the birds sang in chorus to their maker, and the grass glistened with a covering of dew in the early morning hours. The presence of my heavenly Shepherd was so real as I thanked him and praised him for this glorious day. "Wow! Father, I thank you for giving us such a perfect day. Please help me to make the most of it and not waste the time; I have a lot of work to accomplish."

The five lambs grazed contentedly in the pasture, not a care in the world. The grass had grown thick and luscious; the lambs felt safe in their fenced field of grass. When their bellies were full, they would drift to the nearby barn, which shades them from the rising sun. There they found refreshing cold water in the automatic waterer waiting to quench their thirst.

"Well, Lord, since I'm out here enjoying the tranquility of the morning, I might as well check the fence. I do need to make sure there aren't any new holes through which these little guys might escape. Even worse would be an opening through which a dog or coyote might enter the field in quest of a tasty meal, or a morning of fun and games with helpless lambs. I remember when those dogs got into the corral a couple of years ago—what a tragic mess!"

As I strolled along the fence, tightening it up occasionally and pulling out a weed which had grown too large, I enjoyed watching the lambs as they celebrated their awesome morning adventure. Lambs exhibit their joy by leaping in the air, sprinting back and forth, their goal an invisible marker. They "bunny hopped," a term our family coined while watching lambs bounce along with all four feet leaving the ground in unison. Feeling protected and secure in their fenced-in universe, all seemed perfect to the five young lambs.

In the distance I heard the low growl of a tractor rumbling down the gravel road which parallels the pasture's outer boundary. Louder and louder it roared as it approached. Since we are farmers and live out in the country, I barely notice the common occurrence of tractors and other large machines traveling down our roads. And the lambs thought nothing of it either as they were accustomed to hearing the sound from the multitude of large, noisy equipment which passes by every day.

All seemed good until my husband honked the horn and waved to me. The horn honking sent the lambs into a frenzy. Immediately, I found myself being inundated by five frightened lambs who were seeking protection from the huge green monster who squawked at them. Instinctively, they ran to their best chance for protection, the shepherd. It seemed they couldn't get near enough and nearly knocked me over as they crowded against my legs, each one fighting to be the closest.

"Lord, you know how much I am like these lambs. When everything is going well, I get a false sense of security and too much independence; I wallow in the fact that I am doing just great. All my needs are being met, mostly by my own doing. My family makes me proud and happy. At those times I feel thankful. I have health and provision."

At times like these it seems like my world is secure and I can handle whatever might come my way. Sure, there are some minor problems, but nothing I can't overcome with effort or with the help of family and friends. I tend to forget my Shepherd is with me all the time, even though I ignore him or only give him a little bit of my time. He wants to be involved in our lives, every bit of our lives, all the time. Nothing is too small for his concern. Most often I am blind to the fact that he is there protecting me and mending fences so the enemy will be discouraged from sneaking in and taking control of my life.

Like the five lambs, I live in a state of euphoria until suddenly I am faced with a problem beyond my ability to cope. Of course, then I run to the Shepherd where he takes me in his arms and encompasses me with his love and forgiveness. How comforting it is to know the Shepherd is so near and just waiting to help me.

I often hear people say, "There's nothing left to do but pray." Why wait for a crisis to call for God's help? He has promised to never leave us or forsake us. He is always with us and his Word says he will deliver us from fear. After all, it is Jesus who has provided everything we need. And it is he who would love to have us run to him as our Shepherd. He loves us so very much and desires that relationship with us. I think our heavenly Shepherd really likes us to cling to him like the lambs crowding me when they were afraid. I do enjoy it when my lambs show no fear yet stay close to me; I think the Lord feels the same way.

–Millie

To Ponder:

- What circumstances in my life could cause a breach in my relationship with God?
- As I compare my life with the five lambs in the pasture, I ask myself: Am I contented with the way my life is going? What positive things in my life seem to be "luscious grass"?
- How do I run to my Shepherd? Can I feel his love and comfort? His forgiveness?

To Pray:

My Shepherd, thank you for your provision of all my needs and for your protection. Thank you for not providing all my wants, as you know what's best for me. Thank you for always being there and willing to listen to me when I am afraid, and even when I'm not afraid. Please help me remember you are always with me and watching over me as my Shepherd-friend. Forgive me when I fail to run to you for all my needs.

2
Acceptance

To the praise of the glory of His grace, by which He made us accepted in the Beloved.

–Ephesians 1:6 (NKJV)

The soft sound of bleating reached me as I sauntered toward the chicken house turned lambing barn. We had acquired the old egg-producing chicken shed which was a long, low dilapidated building with windows all across the front and remodeled it into the building reserved for our ewes at lambing time. There was room for nine individual pens (or "jugs") and one pen for supplies. Now, instead of the cackling of hens, the old structure was home to the bleating of sheep.

"Charlene! What a lovely baby you have," I exclaimed as I entered the chilly sheep maternity barn on that freezing February morning. My nose wrinkled with the pungent odor of a full, moist barn. "But only one lamb this year? Usually you have twins."

Charlene had become one of my favorites. She was quite smart, in spite of the common thought that all sheep are stupid. She was one of the "dead" sheep that my daughter Shelly and I had rescued from death on a scorching hot summer day several years earlier. She had been thrown out of a feedlot unto the "dead" pile, because she was so sick that the manager of the feedlot thought she was dead. We saw that she was still breathing, and with permission, brought her to our farm, where we nursed her back to health. She had recovered well and seemed to have no permanent problems, so I decided to add her to my band of ewes. It was a good decision; she produced well for several years, often bearing twin lambs.

After bedding down Charlene and her still-wet, white baby with lots of soft yellow straw, I proceeded to check the other mamas. Several more ewes had lambed, and each one had to be moved into an individual pen with her new baby/babies and made comfortable with straw, feed and water. I checked each ewe's bag to ensure she had an udder full of milk. Also, it was important to make sure that each lamb had figured out where its food supply was and that each knew how to drink the thick warm colostrum which is so vital to a healthy start in life. There appeared to be a problem with one mother who had borne twin lambs. She had very little milk. I would need to keep an eye on these lambs to make sure they didn't starve.

Throughout the day, I entered the barn to the welcoming baas of hungry ewes. Little lambs echoed the cries of their mamas, but the plaintive cries of the two revealed that their tummies were nearly empty and they were starving. I checked all the other ewes and lambs; all seemed to be well with them. In a soft voice, I spoke to Charlene, "Charlene, you need to raise twins again this year."

I was certain the ewe that was short on "groceries" would not be able to feed both of her lambs. As a solution, I placed one of the new twins into the pen with Charlene and her new white baby. I gave Charlene the new orphan. This lamb was black. Charlene took one look and said, "Uh, uh, that's not my baby." I was sure she would change her mind in a little while, but by the time I figured there was no hope of reversing Charlene's mind-set, it was too late! Enough of Charlene's strong sheep smell, (an odor belonging to each sheep and detected only by other sheep) had infiltrated the black baby's body so that his birth mother would not take him back. On to the next plan I went. After putting a sheep halter on Charlene's head, I tied her on a fairly short leash in the corner of the lambing jug. She was given a small bucket of water and a flake of hay which she could reach; the short rope allowed her to lie down but limited her moving around. This way, she could not butt, nor smell the unwanted baby and he would have opportunity to eat, without being brutalized.

For several days, I monitored his eating and soon noticed that when it was time for the two babies to eat, Charlene would look lovingly to the left where her own lamb suckled, but when she glanced to the right side where the newcomer was eating, himself oblivious of any problem, Charlene would stomp her front foot and hop around on her back legs. As a general rule, ewes identify their babies by smell, but because of Charlene's limited range of motion there was no way Charlene could distinguish between the two lambs. There was only one answer: Charlene was not color blind! The little black lamb was a determined fellow and was able to get his meals even from an unwilling mother. After a few days, the smell of Charlene's wool and milk saturated his body so that he smelled just like her own lamb, and she decided to accept him as her own in spite of his being born to another ewe. I removed her halter and watched with delight as Charlene nuzzled the black baby as well as her own white baby—a family at last!

As I watched the new, happy sheep family, I thought about how often we as humans discriminate against someone who is different from us. Like Charlene, we are happy with our own lives, and don't want to be bothered with any changes which might interfere with our contentment. There are so many different ways our prejudicial tendencies may manifest themselves, and it is certainly not always connected with skin color. I have been guilty of judging a person's actions as wrong. Maybe their choice of clothing, makeup or hairstyle seems inappropriate, or I don't agree with the way they express themselves. I am embarrassed to admit that, much like Charlene's unwillingness to accept a lamb different from herself, I have let my pettiness interfere with my willingness to accept and love people different from me. Today, my goal is to let the love of God infiltrate me so thoroughly that I become color blind to the faults and differences of others.

I am still working on this, as it is difficult for me to not judge others. Slowly I am finding it easier, and very rewarding, to overlook what I have perceived as faults in others. We do not always agree with the lifestyles of some acquaintances, but we need to love and accept them as they are. As Ephesians 1:6 tells us, Jesus' grace makes us accepted by the Father. If he can accept us with all our faults, who are we to deny acceptance to those with whom we disagree?

–Millie

To Ponder:

- Do I have a tendency to discriminate against others who are "different" than I?
- How would I feel if I had no friends because of the way I dress, the way I wear my hair, the activities I enjoy, where my home is located, etc.?
- Help me think of one person I can befriend and show Christ's love.
- How can I go about being a friend to an unlovable person who seems very lonely?

TO PRAY:

Heavenly Father, thank you for being my Shepherd. Please forgive me when I allow prejudice toward someone who is "different" than I, to influence my attitudes and actions. Thank you for your forgiving grace that accepts me in spite of all my sin. Lead me to those persons you choose—not just those I would choose—for me to befriend, and empower me to share your love with them. Fill my mouth with the words you want me to speak, and open her/his heart to receive them. Thank you, Jesus.

3
Adopted

But when the fullness of the time had come, God sent forth His Son, born of a woman, born under the law, to redeem those who were under the law, that we might receive the adoption as sons.

–Galatians 4:4-5 (NKJV)

With anticipation I stepped out into the frigid night air—so cold I thought I heard the stars twinkling. It was 3:00 a.m. and time for the night check of the ewes who were delivering their lambs.

"Lord, you know how I hate to get up in the middle of the night; you know how I dread facing the cold, but it is beautiful and peaceful. Thank you that I can enjoy this night's extraordinary beauty and tranquility."

Five minutes later, I entered the lambing shed. It reeked of sheep breath, sheep manure, and sheep urine—a drastic change from the fresh air outside. "I've got to clean these jugs out tomorrow before they get worse," I told myself.

And then I noticed the ewe whose delivery had seemed imminent at the 11:00 p.m. "check." She had just given birth to two lambs, but there was a problem. It seemed she was wholeheartedly rejecting one of them. They both looked healthy and seemed to feel like newborn lambs should feel. However, as they struggled to get to their feet, I noticed that one of them was odd looking. In all ways but one, he seemed normal but his mom wanted no part of him. His tail wriggled vigorously as he anticipated his first meal, but he would not get it from this mom. She wanted only a perfect lamb. His problem was too apparent. His back was missing some vertebrae, so he was much shorter in body length than he should have been, resulting in a strange-looking, cumbersome lamb. His mom refused to let him drink of the life-saving milk she needed to provide for him.

"Come on, Mom, you need to feed this baby, too." I tried to coax the ewe, but there was no use. She was not changing her mind.

Just one thing left to do: since she was determined to reject this offspring, I had to find a surrogate mother. Another ewe in the corral had given birth a day before but lost her baby, so after a lengthy chase, I captured her and put her in a jug. She had decided she did not really need the baby she had lost, but as was my practice in difficult cases such as this, I haltered her and tied her on a short leash in the corner. This gave her just enough room to eat, drink, and lie down but could not reach the nursing lamb to butt him away. The little deformed lamb didn't care who wanted to feed him; he just wanted to eat. He lustily drank his first meal.

Shorty was a scrapper and was determined that this "meal table" was his. For a week, he ate and grew. The ewe never accepted the situation, and after the week was up, I resigned myself to having another "bottle baby." When I opened the gate to release the ewe back to the flock she hurriedly took off to join them. Just then my dog ran into the pen to team up with me. Immediately the ewe spun around and dashed back to the barn. What a shock it was to me when she ran into the jug and claimed the weird-looking lamb. The ewe's motherly instinct suddenly overcame her when she saw the dog and knew she needed to protect "her" lamb. She led him out into the corral and from then on, Shorty became her very own baby.

How fortunate we are that God looks not at our abnormalities nor our backgrounds. He loves us just as we are, no matter who we are or what we have done. He does not look at our physical or mental makeup, but when we come to him in repentance and faith, he accepts us unconditionally. Unlike the surrogate ewe in this incident, it does not take a frightening occurrence to goad him into adopting us. He wants to protect us and take care of our needs, feed us through his Word. Most of all, he wants to talk to us and listen to us, and he desires our love. Jesus came to earth to live and die in order that we might be redeemed from our sins and be adopted into his family, to actually become children of the heavenly Father. How awesome is that!

–Millie

TO PONDER:

- What is my attitude toward folks who I do not consider "normal?"
- Will I be like the surrogate mother and try to protect, love and help others who may not appear to be normal; will I help nourish and shield them from "the world" which can be cruel to such people?
- What comes to mind when I consider the fact that Jesus' perfect sacrifice on the cross atones for all my imperfection?

TO PRAY:

Thank you, my Shepherd, for adopting me as your child and a lamb in your flock, and accepting me, abnormalities and all. Give me the grace to accept others who may not appear "normal," and help me to do what I can to nurture and protect them from the cruelties of the world. Help me to see beyond the faults of others and remember that you are working to transform us into your image.

4
All We, Like Sheep

All we like sheep have gone astray; we have turned, every one, to his own way. And the Lord has laid on Him the iniquity of us all.

–Isaiah 53:6 (NKJV)

"Kelly, do you know someone in 4-H who could teach poultry showmanship?"

I was planning our 4-H club's summer Round Robin showmanship clinic. Round Robin is a competition at the end of county fair, where the winners of the showmanship contest in each animal species compete with each other by showing each species. The 4-H'er with the highest overall score wins a nice, embroidered jacket and bragging rights.

Kelly, my oldest daughter, thought for a moment. "What about Caroline?" Caroline, a vivacious and capable teenager, showed sheep and chickens.

I dialed the number for Caroline's mother and she answered. I explained what we needed. "Any chance Caroline could come on Friday evening to teach our 4-H group about showing poultry?"

"Hold on a minute while I ask her." There was a brief pause. "Caroline says that sounds like great fun. What time should we be there?"

I gave her the details and concluded the conversation with, "If there is anything I can do for you, please let me know."

"As a matter of fact, there is."

The quick response surprised me, even caused a bit of apprehension.

"Is there any chance we could bring our lambs out to your house to wean them?"

Caroline and her family lived in one of those sprawling, metro housing developments where houses sat on an acre or two of land.

"Our neighbors are patient with occasional baaing from Caroline's sheep, but I think it is asking too much for them to have to tolerate the noise during weaning time."

During the first week of weaning, lambs and their mothers baa back and forth constantly. "I wouldn't want you to get fined or kicked out of the development."

We chuckled and agreed they would bring the weanling lambs to our farm Friday.

The day of the 4-H Round Robin clinic, Caroline and her family brought their eight prized young ram and ewe lambs out to our place. After the clinic Caroline led the lambs into our pen, so that her sheep and ours could get acquainted. Our sheep sniffed the newcomers. Some of the new lambs tried to get a drink of milk from our ewes, but their action was rewarded with brisk head butts. The newcomers decided on a better plan—look for solid food. They soon found their way to the heavy, wooden feeders, where they nibbled on some leftover stems of hay. As expected, none of the sheep got overly excited, and by evening they were bedded down side by side, chewing their cuds, the picture of contentment.

The next morning, I rushed out to the sheep pen. I could already feel perspiration running down my neck. It was going to be a warm day. I was relieved to see all eight visiting lambs in residence. "You sheep better get out into the pasture and eat, so that you can rest when it gets hot," I told them, as I swung the woven wire gate open wide to let the flock out onto the pasture. In a few weeks, the hot summer days and scant moisture would turn the grass brown; but today the emerald green landscape beckoned the flock.

Several hours later, my outdoor chores complete, I returned to the house to snap green beans. I was standing at my kitchen sink when my daughter Kelly burst inside. "The sheep have returned to the pen, but Caroline's lambs are gone!"

"I'm sure they'll come back soon." I didn't worry overly much, as I knew the tendency of sheep to stay together.

However, when I checked several hours later, the guest lambs were nowhere to be found. We widened our search to our entire seventy-acre pasture. By now, I had locked in my flock, as the sun had begun to set. We still didn't find the weanlings. Panic began to rise. Not only were the lambs very expensive, registered show sheep; they were Caroline's pets. She loved those sheep.

We called neighbors to ask if they had seen the eight weanlings. Nothing. Some of the neighbors volunteered to help in the search, and we were anxious to accept. I got permission to enter and search neighboring pastures. It was now completely dark. Friends sat in our pickup with spotlights, searching and calling for the lambs. Coyotes yelped, reminding us of the weanlings' vulnerability. Others drove the county roads, hoping to find the lambs on or near the roads. I prayed silently—then out loud—for the lambs' safety and that we would find them. Still nothing.

When it was nearly midnight, I decided to call off the search for the night. I was exhausted, more mentally than physically, and I was sure my kindhearted neighbors were anxious to get to bed.

I washed the majority of the dirt and sweat from my face and arms. In bed, I tossed and turned. I thought about the call I would need to make the next morning to Caroline. How would I explain that I had lost her sheep? Shouldn't

I have known this could happen? I continued to pray that God would let the lambs return whole and happy. I think it was nearly morning light when I fell asleep.

The next morning we resumed the search. I made the call to Caroline's home. Her mother was gracious to a fault. I told her we'd continue to search.

Then the phone rang. It was my neighbor Tim, who had not been involved in the search. "Are you missing some sheep? I have some sheep in that low pasture in front of my house. I thought you might know whose sheep they are."

My knees went weak with relief. "How many are there? Are they young? Have they been injured?"

From his description, they looked like Caroline's sheep.

"I'll be there in a minute."

Sure enough, the eight lambs had wondered about a mile away from our place and had bedded down, I supposed for the night, in Tim's pasture. "You are very lucky babies," I told them, as we herded them back to our place. "You could have been ripped apart by coyotes or dogs."

They responded with nonchalance as they meandered through the tall grass across the unfenced fields to our farm. My daughters and I directed them from behind.

I dialed Caroline's phone number and when she answered, my relief spilled out. "I am so relieved. We found your lambs and they are fit as a fiddle."

For the next several days, I kept all the sheep, ours and the new ones, locked in the pen. When I let them out a few days later, I checked often to make sure the new lambs didn't wonder off again. They never again left the flock. Six weeks later, Caroline picked up her weaned lambs.

Later, as I reflected on this traumatic event, I realized that I assumed the new lambs would stay with the flock because my own sheep are terrified of being separated from the full flock. Physical proximity to the flock gives sheep (most sheep, anyway) a sense of security. It is where they feel safe. Yet, these new lambs did not know my sheep. In addition, because the weanlings were pets rather than livestock, they had been desensitized to danger. They no longer possessed the instinctual fear of being separated from the flock. And I imagine, in their minds, the eight of them considered themselves a flock. Neither rogue dogs nor coyotes had ever chased them, so they had no experience or fear of separation from the flock.

We humans often resemble those wayward weanling lambs with no fear of predators. We don't grasp how much danger we place ourselves in when we wander from the protection of God's laws. Eventually, the coyotes or dogs will come for us.

Living outside God's precepts, which are designed to protect us and give us life, can take on many forms: outright rebellion, harboring of bitterness, or refusing to forgive wrongs. I have learned in my own life that sin is never stagnant. If I don't repent and turn from sin, it will grow and eventually overtake me. The weanlings escaped attack despite being outside the pen for one night, but it is unlikely they would have survived had they stayed out all summer. Likewise, when I choose to live outside God's laws by not repenting of my sin, I will suffer the consequences. But thanks be to God who is merciful and will rescue us and restore us when we call to him.

–Marilyn

TO PONDER:

- Am I allowing sin in my life that is exposing me to danger from the evil one?
- Have I, like these weanlings, become oblivious to the danger of wandering away from God's precepts and thus his protection?
- How can I be sure I am fully under God's protection?

TO PRAY:

Thank you, Good Shepherd, for providing a way for me to be fully protected. Give me a desire to devour your Word and to learn your precepts, so that I do not wander away from you. Point out anything in my life that I am doing in rebellion to your laws. Thank you for your love and grace that searched for me when I was lost. I want to live enfolded in your care.

5
Behold the Lamb

The next day John saw Jesus coming toward him and said, "Look, the Lamb of God, who takes away the sin of the world! This is the one I meant when I said, 'A man who comes after me has surpassed me because he was before me.'"

–John 1: 29-30 (NIV)

Why on earth did I agree to an 8:00 a.m. meeting? I muttered as I rushed outside. I planned to feed my sheep then shower and embark on an hour-long drive to meet with a client.

With the day's schedule on my mind, I stepped into the sheep pen. There I found a sixty-pound lamb thrashing about. She appeared to be having a seizure.

My daughters had left for school, so I had to roll the lamb from its side to its tummy by myself. It was Foxy Lady's baby. Foxy Lady was a favorite of my older daughter, Kelly. We had purchased her as a lamb the previous spring from a neighboring farm. Kelly showed her at the county fair and placed high in a very competitive class. After the fair, Foxy Lady had joined our breeding flock.

What could be wrong? The lamb had looked as fit as a fiddle the day before. I checked her body for signs of trauma, but found nothing. She continued to seize, tossing her head back and her legs to the side.

Just a few days earlier, this ewe lamb had caught my eye. She was growing fast and looked robust. She had a strong, straight topline (back) and good leg and loin muscling. Her legs were straight and she moved gracefully, forecasting many years of soundness as a breeding ewe. She had a certain sass and head carriage about her that indicated she might be a challenge to train for show, but that sassiness was good because it would attract the attention of the judge.

Now I was beginning to panic. I had to do something with the seizing lamb, but I was already running late. Since this was before we had cell phones, I had no way to contact the client to let them know I would be late. I grabbed the ailing lamb around the girth and half-carried, half-dragged her into a small pen. I propped her up against the side of the pen, since lying on the back or the side is hard on a sheep's internal organs. All I had time to do was place her so she wouldn't be trampled.

I was ten minutes late to the meeting. "I am so sorry to have held you up, but this morning when I went to do my chores, I found a lamb in a seizure, and I had to tend to her before I could leave," I attempted to explain to my city client.

Later, when I returned home, the seizures had lessened, but the lamb still couldn't move on her own. She was stretched out on her side, stiff and unresponsive. I debated with myself about putting her down, but decided to give her a bit more time. I again propped her up to the stomach position and offered her hay and water. She was eager to eat and drink—a very good sign! Over the next three days, Kelly or I hand fed and watered her multiple times each day (and night).

On day four, the seizures had quit and she could lie normally. Soon she could reach the food and water we placed near her. At this point, I rigged a belly gurney and simple pulley system to hoist her up into a standing position. She could not support herself. But when she paddled her legs, she got some exercise and strengthened her balance.

Kelly and I spent time helping her stand, and stretching and moving her legs—ovine physical therapy, if you will.

After about ten days, the ewe lamb could walk. At first, she careened comically about the pen. Finally her balance and strength improved to the degree that she could return to the flock. A month after I found her seizing, she looked as though nothing had ever happened to her. Her sass returned, and my daughter even showed this lamb at the county fair.

This experience with Foxy Lady's lamb demonstrates to me both the fragility and resilience of sheep. The lamb was perfectly fine one day and on death's door the next. Yet the lamb also demonstrated incredible resilience by fully recovering from this devastating ailment. When John the Baptist declared Jesus the Lamb of God that takes away the sin of the world, he declared him both a fragile, yielding sacrifice and a resilient, eternal conqueror of sin and evil.

At the time of Jesus' incarnation, the Jews and many other religions practiced animal sacrifice. I believe that God made man with the innate understanding that he is sinful and that sin must be atoned for in a significant manner, even by blood. The Jewish sacrificial system was given by God through Moses with great specificity; yet that was only a forerunner. The lamb sacrifice was a symbol of the final, complete, and efficacious sacrifice yet to come.

The Jewish leaders in Jesus' time were not looking for a Messiah described as a lamb. A lamb, in their eyes, was fragile. Jesus was the Lamb of God who would take away the sin of the world, yet they wanted a Messiah who would free them from their social bondage. They refused to see the strength of the lamb that would free them from spiritual bondage. Jesus came to set their souls free; yet all they looked for was political freedom.

I observe that people today who come in contact with Jesus the Messiah are much the same. They want Jesus to do things for them, to make their lives better and more comfortable, but they do not look to him to transform their souls.

–Marilyn

To Ponder:

- What do people want from Jesus? What do I want him to do for me?
- Do I truly believe that atonement for my sin was completed with Jesus' sacrifice as the Lamb of God or do I try to contribute to the sacrifice through my own efforts and good works?
- If not works, then what is our part in receiving God's gift of salvation?

To Pray:

Father God, thank you for your great sacrifice in sending your Son to die to save us from sin. Thank you that you came as a lamb, both fragile and conqueror. I know there is absolutely nothing I can do to erase my sin and save my soul. You did it all. I choose to accept this incredible gift of salvation and place my faith in you as my Savior and Lord.

Lambs are fragile, but amazingly resilient.

Sheep are defenseless creatures.

6
ICE BABY

What man of you, having a hundred sheep, if he loses one of them, does not leave the ninety-nine in the wilderness, and go after the one which is lost until he finds it? And when he has found it, he lays it on his shoulders, rejoicing. And when he comes home, he calls together his friends and neighbors, saying to them, 'Rejoice with me, for I have found my sheep which was lost!' I say to you that likewise there will be more joy in heaven over one sinner who repents than over ninety-nine just persons who need no repentance.

–Luke 15:4-7 (NKJV)

Even the sheep knew a storm was on the way that afternoon as they returned to the safety of the corral earlier than usual. They had stuffed themselves with tidbits in the hay field where they grazed in the winter months. I watched the ewes and their lambs dutifully enter the corral; it seemed like everybody was home. Still, I scanned the field. But I couldn't see any stragglers.

"Marvin, do you think everybody is in?" I shouted to my husband over the impending roar of the winter storm which was arriving with a fury.

"I don't see any more sheep out there. I think they are all in. Let's hurry up and get the chores done so we can get inside," was his reply. "I think this storm is going to be a dilly, the way it's starting out."

I locked the gate then, not so much to keep the storm out, but to keep the sheep in.

The Bible speaks frequently about the sheepfold, the gate, the rod, and shepherds. In ancient Israel, the sheepfold was a corral with fairly high sides for protection from wild animals. The gate was quite narrow, probably allowing only one or two sheep at a time to pass through it. Usually, several shepherds kept their sheep in one large sheepfold, and when a shepherd and his sheep returned to the fold for the evening, he would lay his rod, or staff, across the doorway, so the sheep had to jump over the rod, one at a time. As the sheep entered the fold, the shepherd could count them, making sure all were present.

The gate to our corral is very wide, and it is nearly impossible to count a large number of sheep passing through it at one time. (Interestingly, when sheep pass through an opening, they nearly always jump through it even though there is no rod lying across the doorway.) We had about ninety ewes at the time, but since it was lambing season, there were quite a few babies entering with their moms. Not long after we had secured everything for the night, the impending blizzard arrived in all its rage. We relaxed, believing all our sheep were safely sheltered from the wrath of a January blizzard.

The next morning as the snow and wind abated, we trudged out to the corral to do chores. There, standing outside the gate, was one lone ewe waiting to be let in. Remnants of afterbirth indicated she had given birth recently, but she had no lamb with her. When I opened the gate to let her in, she made a beeline for the water. We had missed her in our field check the evening before. But could her newborn baby possibly have survived the furious winter storm and the sub-zero temperatures? How could we even find it in the drifts of snow?

Like the shepherd in our Bible verse, we had to try. Marvin jumped on our big black mare, Mecca, and headed out to the field, searching for a newborn baby lamb. We weren't very hopeful that the little one could be found in all the snow drifts, much less that it might have survived the freezing cold and bitter wind. Marvin and Mecca slowly crossed back and forth across the field searching for what seemed like a needle in a haystack. At the far end of the field stood a stack of baled hay, and as he neared the stack, Marvin noticed a lump in the snow. An abundance of snow lumps had been left by the storm, but this particular bump had a tiny hole out of which steam was rising. My husband jumped off of Mecca and when he approached the odd-looking lump, he saw that lump was, in fact, a newborn lamb covered with ice. The ice covering had protected the baby from freezing, and his warm breath had melted the little breathing hole through his frozen covering. What a miracle!

Marvin carefully lifted the lamb, ensconced in a brick of ice, up on Mecca's back as he mounted his horse for the ride home. He was nearly delirious with delight as he shouted, "I found him, and he's OK, but he's really cold!"

Immediately after their arrival, we put the little one in a warm tub of water, continuing to warm the water as we massaged the frigid little body. When he quit shivering, we laid him on a towel, dried him off, and used the hair dryer to finish removing any moisture and warm him up. It wasn't long before he struggled to his feet and began to look for something to eat, bumping and butting my leg while softly bleating for his mom. At that point, we carried the lamb out to the barn and put him under a heat lamp in the lambing pen where his mother awaited her new baby. What a happy reunion!

Likewise, God is delighted when one of his children who has gone astray returns to the fold. Though he has many lambs in his fold, he always searches for any who are lost. What rejoicing in Heaven there is when one of those lost ones is found. He grieves for even one child who has left the safety of the pen. His fold is big enough to hold everyone. Even when we try to hide, the Good Shepherd has no trouble finding us. There are times when we have wandered so far, it is like we are encased with an unpenetratable sheet of ice, but our Shepherd will bring us home, melt the ice, and warm our hearts again. Home is such a secure and comforting place.

–Millie

To Ponder:

- Am I excited to be the Good Shepherd's lamb, to belong in his fold?
- How does the Good Shepherd feel if I turn my back on him and leave his fold?
- Is there anything I might do to make my Shepherd not want me back?
- Think about what it means for my Shepherd to "lay me on his shoulders" and carry me back to the fold. Why would he do that?
- Consider the Lord's sheepfold. Why would it have high walls? Why would he want me to jump over a "staff" to enter?

To Pray:

How grateful I am, Heavenly Shepherd, that you want me in your sheepfold. It is comforting to know that you will come looking for me if I stray. I know I do stray often because I am a human who is so far from perfect. Your blood, shed on the cross, paid the ransom for all my faults. Thank you, Master Shepherd. Even though you have many lambs, you know my name and everything about me. You love me as an individual. Please protect me with high walls and melt any sheets of ice I have around me so I can live to serve you.

7
THE GOOD SHEPHERD WANTS YOUR HEART

I bring no charges against you concerning your sacrifices or concerning your burnt offerings, which are ever before me. I have no need of a bull from your stall or of goats from your pens, for every animal of the forest is mine, and the cattle on a thousand hills. I know every bird in the mountains, and the insects in the fields are mine. If I were hungry I would not tell you, for the world is mine, and all that is in it.

–Psalm 50:8-12 (NIV)

One June we had a family reunion in Steamboat Springs, Colorado. Known for its skiing and outdoor summer sports, the mountain region of Steamboat Springs also has a thriving ranching industry. As we wound our way to and from the mountain resort town, we took in the rich, emerald carpet of grass that wrapped the mountains, hills, and valleys. (In Colorado, where valleys sit 5,000 feet above sea level, we have a "high standard" for what constitutes a hill or mountain.) Clear, bubbling streams tumbled through valley floors.

What plump, healthy animals these pastures must produce, I observed as the road snaked through the hills. Herds of cattle and horses, interspersed with flocks of sheep, were everywhere.

"Look at that!" my mother exclaimed, as we came upon a flock of three to four thousand sheep grazing close to the road. The flock, or perhaps it was two different flocks, grazed on both sides of the road. We slowed to take in the scene. The white-faced, heavy-wooled sheep stood out distinctly on the lush, dark green grass. Smaller balls of wool told me the flock had just lambed. A single-room, portable shepherd's hut sat amid the flock. On the south side of the road, men and women mounted on horses rode through the flock, their eyes peeled for trouble.

On the other side, a shepherd on foot directed alert herding dogs to gather animals that had strayed too far from the flock. The herding dogs—there were three of them—circled around the outside of the wayward sheep. The energetic dogs ran at the stragglers and nipped at their heels to accomplish the goal of sending them back to the flock. On both sides of the road large, long-haired, protection dogs lumbered through the flock. In contrast to herding dogs, protection dogs bond with the sheep and ward off dogs, coyotes, wolves or other predators that threaten the flock. To the untrained eye, they look like big, lazy pets. Not so.

As I surveyed the almost innumerable dots of white, I was reminded of Psalm 50, which tells me the Great Shepherd owns the cattle on a thousand hills. Of course, the psalmist does not record this as a literal statement. He is telling us that God owns the cattle and the sheep and everything else in the entire world. Now that is an impressive spread!

Making an impression, however, was not his purpose in telling me or the Israelites that he owned it all. God's chosen people had become caught up doing the right thing as far as God's laws were concerned, but they were doing it for the wrong reasons. They were bringing the right sacrifices at the right time, as prescribed by Old Testament law; yet God was not pleased.

I raise sheep for the purpose of providing meat to customers, yet driving a group of market ready lambs to the meat processing plant is something I do not like. I research the plant I use and ensure that slaughter is humane. I am comforted knowing my lambs lead a very pleasant life. But, the fact is, they are born and raised to provide meat. Because I really love my sheep, I find the sacrificial system established by God difficult. I am very glad I live and practice my Christian faith after Christ's final and ultimate sacrifice on the cross, which closed the chapter of animal sacrifice. Yet, as difficult as it may sometimes be, it is really important that modern day Christians study and understand the significance of the Old Testament sacrificial system. These laws, given by God to Moses for our spiritual ancestors, the Israelites, are worthy of study today.

Hebrews 9:22 tells us that without the shedding of blood there is no remission of sins. Remission is another word for forgiveness. The obligatory shedding of animal blood was instituted by God to show humankind, from the Hebrews in the wilderness to us today, the seriousness of sin. Even pagans intuitively understood this. Most ancient civilizations, from the Vikings in northern Europe to the Aztecs in Mexico, had some form of animal or human sacrifice. Animal sacrifices ordained by God also were meant to point people to Jesus Christ and his ultimate and final sacrifice. He wanted them to understand the severity of sin and that their sin would be paid for by a perfect, innocent lamb, the Lamb of God.

The problem with the people to whom this psalm is addressed is that they were simply going through the motions of worship without giving the Lord their hearts. Sadly, many today do the same. We go to church, sing songs, and help out other people if required. We may even pray before meals and have family devotions. God never wanted the Israelites nor does he want Christians today to ever get to a point where faith is a list of obligations. Rather, he wants me to experience the joy of a relationship with the Creator of the universe.

Dutifully doing what is expected of me is not a bad thing in and of itself. But merely going through the motions is not what God wants of me. Until I give my heart to the Lord and find joy in my relationship with him, I cannot please my Good Shepherd, who is the ultimate sacrifice for all humankind.

How do I find or renew the joy in my relationship with the Good Shepherd?

Some time ago, my eyes were opened to the legalism in the lives of some people who were close to me. They were more concerned with appearances than with the reality of their relationship. I told God I did not want to be like this. I wanted to have a genuine relationship with him. I began to ask him how to please him. It is a prayer God is glad to hear. Over time, he has changed my heart to truly love and serve him.

–Marilyn

To Ponder:

- What might be our modern-day equivalent of "sacrifices and burnt offerings" as referred to in Psalm 50:8?
- In what ways might I merely be "going through the motions?"
- If my relationship has become a list of do's and don'ts, how can I turn it back to the relationship God intended for me?

TO PRAY:

Thank you, Father, for sending your Son, the perfect Lamb of God to be the final sacrifice for humankind. I am so thankful that I can have a relationship with you through your Son's finished work on the cross. Help me never to take this for granted, nor to lose the joy of my salvation. Let me not slip into complacency and go through the motions of being religious simply to show others my faith. Let my faith always be real, vibrant, and active. Take my heart, it is yours.

Sheep stay together for protection.

8
Restoration

Create in me a clean heart, O God, and renew a steadfast spirit within me. Do not cast me away from Your presence, and do not take Your Holy Spirit from me. Restore to me the joy of Your salvation, and uphold me by Your generous Spirit.

–Psalm 51:10-12 (NKJV)

"Do you know there is a sheep walking down the road?" quizzed a friend of mine who had just arrived for an afternoon visit.

"Oh, my goodness, no; I'd better go and catch it," I responded as I headed for the door. "I'll be right back, I hope; make yourself at home."

I rushed out the back door, leaving my guest behind, then raced to the only vehicle in sight. The old Ford station wagon struggled to wake up but finally roared into action, and down the dirt road we flew, flinging dirt and gravel in all directions. It took less than a minute to overtake the runaway ewe, who had managed to travel more than a half mile from our home. At a glance I could see it was Scotch, an independent Southdown ewe who definitely had a mind of her own. Not only was Scotch on the road, but she had also enticed her favorite baby to join her as they sought greener pastures.

Several weeks before, Scotch had given birth to a set of twins. From the very start, she had chosen a favorite baby, and although she wasn't fond of her second child, she dutifully, though begrudgingly, allowed him to eat at mealtimes.

She was obviously unhappy about feeding the less favorite lamb. She lovingly nuzzled her favored baby, but as she turned her head to see who was eating on the other side, and her eyes caught sight of the unloved one, she stomped a foot in ruthless disgust at having to submit to this child's whims. But her motherly sense of obligation compelled her to take care of him. As he grew, I no longer worried I'd have an orphan lamb to raise.

But the day had come when Scotch decided she'd had enough. She gathered up her favorite infant, sought a route of escape, and the two of them left the rest of the flock behind, including her unloved baby who hadn't yet missed his mama. (I never did find their escape route.) As I raced down the road in hot pursuit of the two runaways, my mind reviewed the setup of the corral, trying to figure out where the "hole" was. They had out-foxed me.

I drove alongside the two, pulled ahead, parked the car, opened the back door and said, "Get in, Scotch."

After I put the baby inside, Scotch looked at me rather disgustedly and laboriously climbed into the back seat of the station wagon. Her plans had been foiled. Home we came. Scotch and her lamb climbed out of the car and I herded them into the corral via the gate. As Scotch and her beloved baby reluctantly entered the corral, the unloved one came running up, bleating as though to say, "Where were you, Mom? I missed you, but I'm glad you are back."

My friend was patiently waiting for me when I returned to the house. As we enjoyed our afternoon coffee, I shared my story of the runaway sheep with her. I was so appreciative that she had noticed the animals trotting down the road that afternoon.

Of the hundreds of sheep I have owned, I believe Scotch was my favorite. I find great joy in remembering her escapades. Scotch never escaped nor ran away again, and she dutifully raised both lambs. Just think how delighted our heavenly Shepherd is when we return "home" from a wayward ordeal which breaks his heart. He will hunt us down and take us back. He never casts us out and is always willing to forgive us and renew our relationship with him. What a blessing it is to be restored to relationship with our heavenly Father after we have strayed away!

–Millie

To Ponder:

- Do I tend to look for "breaches in the fence" where I can escape the watchful eyes of my Shepherd?
- Is there someone or something in my life that is causing me to stray? What should I do about it?
- Is it difficult for me to "return to the fold" when I am caught looking for "greener grass?"
- Do I have friends who will confront me when I am straying?

To Pray:

Thank you, Heavenly Father, for keeping your eyes on me, especially when I stray from the fold. Please help me to be aware that I must not allow myself, or influence others, to wander away. Help me find contentment when I am safely in your keeping, and guide me away from activities which are not pleasing to you. Thank you for the unspeakable joy of belonging to you.

9
Stay With the Flock

And let us consider how we may spur one another on towards love and good deeds, not giving up meeting together, as some are in the habit of doing, but encouraging one another—and all the more as you see the Day approaching.

–Hebrews 10:24-25 (NIV)

I head out on a spring morning to do my early chores. Today I start a new feeding routine. Just before breeding and again three to four months before the time when the lambs are born—this is called lambing season—I add corn to the ewes' diet of hay and pasture to give them a little extra energy. It is not an entirely new routine, but they haven't had corn since the previous fall.

When the ewes see me coming, they move toward the hay feeder inside their pen and greet me with anticipation. Instead of giving them hay as usual, though, I grab a five gallon bucket and place it under the granary that stands off the ground on four sturdy metal legs. It has a small door underneath, and when I open it, the corn falls fast. I slam the door shut. With a partial bucket of corn, I head to the feeding area outside of, and adjacent to, the ewe's pen. I evenly distribute the corn between the pans, piquing the interest of the ewes.

My woolly girls, watching me closely, seem to realize their hay is not forthcoming. I can see them fishing into their memory banks of how they get to their meal. To reach the corn, they'll have to go out the gate on the opposite side and go around to where the pans of corn await them. I move to the gate and wait until all the ewes are crowded against it. If I open the gate too soon, most will run out, but the stragglers will panic and not see where the rest of the flock have gone. Sheep become uneasy when they are scattered or separated. Today I am patient, remembering that waiting until all the ewes are ready to leave together will, in the long run, save time and yield better results.

I fling open the gate. They hesitate for a second then pour out the gate and around the outside of the pen in one big rush of wool on feet, and eat the corn. As soon as they finish, most run back into the pen to wait for me to feed them hay. There are a few stragglers, the clean-your-plate types who take longer to return. Soon all are back in the pen.

My years of shepherding have taught me that sheep hate to be alone, especially when in a new situation or environment. Unlike cattle, which respond well to being aggressively pushed from behind by someone they don't know, sheep try to run back to the place they came from. Sheep must be led or pushed gently and with minimal pressure by someone they know. They need time to assess the safety of the new place. Often the most effective method of moving sheep is when the shepherd strides out ahead of them. They will follow—as a group. The larger the flock, the safer the sheep feel. Shepherds call this preference or tendency to group together "flocking."

In the spring when I turn the flock out to pasture, the sheep run out as a group and stay in a group until they return home, either because they are spooked or because it is time to drink and rest. Not long ago, I looked out my window and saw my flock crowded together in the open-sided shed, staring out at something. I turned to see what they were looking at, and there, across the field, sauntered a coyote.

When pastured sheep feel no danger lurking, they spread out and graze, but at the slightest hint of danger, they group together so tightly, one can hardly distinguish individual animals within the flock. This is an instinctual response, God's provision for these helpless creatures. If a sheep breaks from the flock and runs, a predator can easily see it and pick it off.

Stupid sheep, you say? Maybe; but if you consider that sheep have no natural defense—they can't run fast, kick or bite—it makes sense for them to group together as a defense against predators.

Before I understood a sheep's instinctual urge to stay with other sheep, I tried to push individual animals into a new place or one they had not used in a long time by pressuring them from behind. It was frustrating and ineffective. I have learned to give them hours or even days to check out the new environment before moving them. Now none of them panic, and they all move together into the new space.

It occurred to me one day, after spending an unsuccessful hour trying to move a group of sheep to a new place, that a sheep's instinct to "flock" with other sheep for safety is an excellent example of why believers need each other's fellowship. Looking to other Christians for instruction and fellowship is my God-given safety net. The importance of discernment notwithstanding, believers who value their independence to the degree that they don't mind hanging out by themselves are more vulnerable to the negative influences of the world and attacks from the evil one. Hanging with a flock of believers is my protection.

I empathize with those who say they don't want to attend church or Bible studies or socialize with other Christians because they have been "burned" by church people. Others justify their absence by claiming they get more out of being with nature on weekend camping trips than they get from fellowship with other believers.

Ultimately, we must recognize our Lord's admonition that we are to worship with and learn from other believers. Sheep know this instinctively. Christians need to learn the importance of having a strong spiritual and social network. A good model is for each follower of Christ to be discipled by a strong, growing believer or group of believers, then for each person to aspire to grow to the point that he or she can disciple new Christians.

God has no grandchildren. Each of us in his or her own right must become a son or daughter of our heavenly Father. However, the Lord provides us with brothers and sisters in Christ to help us grow and enjoy safe pasture as we traverse this path of life.

–Marilyn

To Ponder:

- How can I better allow fellow Christians to speak truth into my life?
- How can I better follow the Lord's mandate to spur others on to love and good deeds?
- How can I today encourage a brother or sister in Christ?

To Pray:

Mighty Shepherd, thank you for giving me brothers and sisters in Christ with whom I can fellowship, grow in faith, and learn how to live for you. Show me how to encourage others and spur them on to love and good deeds. Give the wisdom and discernment to find straying Christians and bring them back into the safety of the flock. Instill in me a humble heart to receive encouragement and admonition from my fellow believers. Empower me with your grace to put aside the hurts caused by other Christians, the hurts that may have hindered my fellowship with the body of Christ. Put in my path those who need me and to whom I can minister. Bring to mind people who need my help.

Sheep hear very well but must be trained to listen and respond to the shepherd's voice

Typically, sheep are color blind.

10
A Keen Sense of Hearing

To him the doorkeeper opens, and the sheep hear his voice; and he calls his own sheep by name and leads them out. And when he brings out his own sheep, he goes before them; and the sheep follow him, for they know his voice. . . . . My sheep hear My voice, and I know them, and they follow Me.

–John 10:3-4, 27 (NKJV)

"Shannon, come quick," I hollered into the house from the back door. "Two of the lambs didn't come in. It's almost dark, and I need your help—now!"

"Where are they?" Shannon ambled out, severely lacking the urgency I felt.

"At first I thought they got picked off by coyotes, but now I see them across the fence in Sarah's pasture." I needed my young, fit daughter to go to the neighbor's pasture and herd the vagrants back home to safety. "I can see them pacing the fence." I squinted and pointed toward our north fence line, where the lambs were stranded. "They must not be able to figure out how to get back into our pasture."

"I got it, Mom." She shouted over her shoulder as she trotted off toward the lambs, our herding dog, Freckles, at her side.

Five minutes later, I could see Shannon drop to all fours. She and Freckles scooted under the fences and began to whoop and holler at the stranded sheep. The pressure pushed them back through the "hole" through which they had escaped. They were soon running for the barn, Freckles on their heels.

"Thanks, Shannon, you're a real trooper," I said when she was within earshot. "I was worried we lost two lambs."

"No problem, Mom." Nonchalant, she headed for the house.

Why couldn't they just come running in when I call them—like their mothers do? Of course I knew the answer. They were not yet trained to hear and respond to their shepherd's voice.

Because of their keen sense of hearing and sensitivity to danger, sheep can be trained to come in from pasture when the shepherd calls. My flock of ewes, most of which were born on my farm and range in age from two to ten, are very easy to manage on pasture. I let them out in the morning to graze. They stay together and return to the corral several times each day to drink water and to rest. Sheep prefer to graze in the early morning or evening, especially on hot days. During midday, they can often be found resting in the loafing shed, enjoying the cool breezes that flow through the barn and attached loafing shed. By dusk, they will be back inside the safety of the corral, or if not, when I call, they will come.

When I have more than one group of sheep to graze, I must split the time each group is out on the pasture. Once the lambs are weaned and have their own, separate pen next to the ewe pen, I cannot let the ewes and lambs graze together, because I feed them differently. The lambs (teenagers in human terms) get unlimited feed for good growth. The ewes, however, only need enough feed to regain their condition once the lambs are weaned. Unlimited feeding is not only wasteful; it makes the ewes over fat.

From the time the lambs are weaned in early summer until they are sold in fall, I turn out the ewes in the morning and lock them up midday. Then, I turn out the lambs to graze from midday until evening. The ewes are easy to manage on pasture, but the lambs must be trained to return when I call them.

When the lambs are weaned and start grazing pasture by themselves, I put green, leafy hay in their feeders to lure them back to the pen. Then I call them, so that they get used to my voice. Initially, the lambs ignore my voice, because prior to this, all they have done is follow their mothers. When they ignore me, I walk out into the 70-acre pasture where they are grazing, still calling them. With the help of our Freckles, I shoo them back into the pen. Freckles enjoys nipping at their heels to send them running toward the barn. This follows for several days, sometimes weeks until finally they see me coming and, without being chased, move toward the pen. Usually, their trek home is circuitous, as they stop to nibble bits of grass here or run yonder to see what is under a bush.

Inevitably, one or more lambs will decide to explore the road or the pasture beyond their own pasture, and either my daughter or I must chase them back into our pasture and to their pen. But, eventually, they all learn to hear and respond to my voice.

A month after the two lambs got stranded in my neighbor's pasture, my sister was visiting and offered to help me with my evening chores.

"That would be great," I told her. "Would you walk out into the pasture and call the lambs like this?: 'Here lambs, here lambs.'" I demonstrated the voice command I use to call my sheep.

"Here lambs, here lambs." She called repeatedly. But the lambs ignored her.

As I filled the ewe and lamb feeders with hay, I watched as my sister circled behind the lambs, Freckles at her side. Only then did the lambs begin to amble off, vaguely in the direction of the barn. No urgency.

How irritating. They had been coming in just fine with my voice command. "Here lambs, here lambs," I belted out from the barn.

Immediately, the heads of the lambs shot up in attention. Moments later, they bolted for the pen at a dead run.

"They sure do know your voice." My sister returned, panting, from her sheep herding adventure.

There is probably no one whose voice sounds more like mine than my sister's, yet the lambs could tell the difference. They ignored her voice but recognized mine and obeyed with haste. I thought about this in relation to John chapter 10, which tells us we should hear and heed the voice of our Shepherd. We should be tone deaf to any other shepherd who calls us, but ready and willing to follow the voice of the one and only Good Shepherd.

Just as my lambs take time and training to hear and come to my voice, we as believers have to learn to hear and obey the voice of our Good Shepherd. When we repent of our sins and ask Jesus to be our Savior, the Holy Spirit comes into our lives. He whispers direction, but it takes time for us to learn to listen to the still, small voice of the Shepherd. Fortunately, he is infinitely patient in teaching us to know his voice.

–Marilyn

To Ponder:

- How well do I know the Great Shepherd's voice?
- When I hear his call, do I obey?
- Have I experienced the comfort of running to him for guidance and protection?

- Why does it take time to learn to hear the call of the Good Shepherd?
- How can I be more responsive to hear and respond to his call?

To Pray:

Thank you, Good Shepherd, for calling me to yourself. Teach me to have ears that are sensitive to your voice. Help me to grow and become a mature sheep in your flock, rather than a flighty lamb that doesn't know you are calling me for protection and nourishment. Thank you for assuring me that you call because you love me and want to guide and protect me.

Twin registered Southdowns, just a few days old

11
A Lamb Called 'Her'

He was oppressed and afflicted, yet he did not open his mouth; he was led like a lamb to the slaughter, and as a sheep before its shearers is silent, so he did not open his mouth.

–Isaiah 53:7 (NIV)

"Shannon, would you please check the ewes to see if any have lambed or are in labor?" I was preparing food for a noon potluck. I turned to my younger daughter. "Take a good look at Mary. She didn't come to the feeder when I gave the ewes their hay this morning." Not eating is one of several signs that a ewe is starting labor.

"Sure, Mom." The back door clunked closed. Shannon was especially interested because Mary was the offspring of a registered Southdown show ewe that Shannon had purchased three years earlier as a 4-H project.

She was back in a few minutes. "Mary has a baby, a ewe lamb, and it is sooo cute."

"Is the lamb healthy?" I spooned fruit salad into a serving dish and popped it into the refrigerator. "Did you put Mary and the baby in a jug?"

"Yeah, Mom, the lamb is fine. I put them in the jug with clean straw and gave Mary a bucket of water." Shannon paused. "The lamb is really short, though."

"Southdowns are short, Shannon."

"No, Mom, I mean really short."

This piqued my curiosity. I pulled on my overalls and slipped on my chore boots, then hurried out to the barn.

Sure enough. There stood Mary, looking like the proud mama she was. Her lamb had a stocky build and the cutest, wool-covered face, but the baby's legs were about half the normal length—not much longer than those of a Dachshund or a Corgi dog. This was the first dwarf sheep in my flock.

Both Shannon and her older sister, Kelly, became enthralled with this ewe lamb. "We decided to name her Her," Shannon announced the next day.

"What?" I was confused.

"You know how you are always nagging us and correcting our grammar?" Kelly had a mischievous glint in her eye. "This is how we are going to get back at you."

"We can say 'Her is so cute.' and 'Her needs to be fed." Shannon laughed at her joke. "And you can't correct us, Mom."

I had two inventive daughters. It was all in good fun. Her was indeed cute, sweet and calm. The girls would take Her out of the pen when she got a little older and play with her. She followed them around like a puppy. She enjoyed the handfuls of grain the girls gave her but was never pushy about it. Her's mother, Mary, also an easy-going, trusting ewe, wasn't the type to fret.

Her epitomized a sheep's natural gentleness and meekness. When pulled out of the flock for shearing, sheep will fight being held on the ground because they are scared, but no sound comes from their mouths. Not everyone believes sheep are "dumb" or stupid (that is the subject of another story); but one thing everyone who has spent time around sheep will agree on is that they are gentle, unassuming creatures.

Sheep in general and Her in particular bring to mind this scripture from Isaiah. In his final hours, Jesus faced his accusers without argument. Scriptural accounts of his trial and persecution tell us he made no attempt to save himself or to argue his innocence. His gentleness at trial fulfilled the Scripture inspired by the Holy Spirit and written by the prophet Isaiah centuries before Jesus walked the earth. Jesus knew he would be falsely condemned and that he would be tortured to death.

Jesus was not gentle and submissive to evil. His overturning the money changers' tables outside the temple comes to mind. But throughout his trial and crucifixion he behaved like a lamb. He was submitting, instead, to the Father and willingly offering himself. Isaiah 53:10 says "It pleased the Lord to bruise him." It pleased the Lord because God the Father knew Jesus' sacrifice would provide the perfect and final sacrifice to cover humankind's transgressions and to provide a way to reconcile us with our heavenly Father.

–Marilyn

To Ponder:

- Why did Jesus act differently in each circumstance? For example, why would he act very aggressively in one situation, such as overturning the money changers tables, and then not even speak to defend himself during his trial?
- Was he being inconsistent?
- How do I apply this approach to conflict in my own life?

TO PRAY:

Good Shepherd, I ask for wisdom and discernment to be able to act and react in ways that are pleasing to you. May I follow the guidance and teaching of the Holy Spirit every day, as I learn to live as you would have me live. Help me handle conflict and disappointment in a way that honors you. Remind me that your ways are higher than man's ways. Help me choose your ways over my own ways.

Some ewes, such as the one here, can feed triplets, while in other cases, one of the triplets becomes a bottle baby.

12
GOAT OR SHEEP?

All the nations will be gathered before him, and he will separate the people one from another as a shepherd separates the sheep from the goats. He will put the sheep on his right and the goats on his left. Then the King will say to those on his right, 'Come, you who are blessed by my Father; take your inheritance, the kingdom prepared for you since the creation of the world. For I was hungry and you gave me something to eat, I was thirsty and you gave me something to drink, I was a stranger and you invited me in, I needed clothes and you clothed me, I was sick and you looked after me, I was in prison and you came to visit me.' Then the righteous will answer him, 'Lord, when did we see you hungry and feed you, or thirsty and give you something to drink? When did we see you a stranger and invite you in, or needing clothes and clothe you? When did we see you sick or in prison and go to visit you?' The King will reply, 'Truly I tell you, whatever you did for one of the least of these brothers and sisters of mine, you did for me.' Then he will say to those on his left, 'Depart from me, you who are cursed, into the eternal fire prepared for the devil and his angels. For I was hungry and you gave me nothing to eat, I was thirsty and you gave me nothing to drink, I was a stranger and you did not invite me in, I needed clothes and you did not clothe me, I was sick and in prison and you did not look after me.' They also will answer, 'Lord, when did we see you hungry or thirsty or a stranger or needing clothes or sick or in prison, and did not help you?' He will reply, 'Truly I tell you, whatever you did not do for one of the least of these, you did not do for me.' Then they will go away to eternal punishment, but the righteous to eternal life.

–Matthew 25:32-46 (NIV)

"Bottle lambs. So cute but so much work," I grumbled as I mechanically completed the twice-a-day ritual of blending dried-milk powder with warm water in my kitchen blender and then pouring the lamb milk replacer through a plastic funnel into individual feeding bottles. Try as I might not to make a mess, drops of the thick, sticky mixture dot my floor and counter. The counter around the blender is covered in a coat of residual milk powder that puffed out the top of the blender rather than surrendering to the whirling blades that sucked most of the powder into the warm water.

Make lamb milk, clean my kitchen, feed the lambs their bottles, wash the bottles—a never ending cycle. "There's got to be a better way," I muttered, heading out to the barn with two bottles of lamb milk under my right arm.

Long before I reached the barn door, I heard the bottle lambs asking for their breakfast. My grumpiness dissipated the moment I opened the gate inside the barn and spied the three lambs running toward me. Squirt was the smallest of a set of triplets. His mother rejected him outright, probably because her innate sense told her she would be unable to feed three lambs. He ate with gusto, butting the bottle, the instinctive way lambs coax out more milk from a ewe's udder. The other two unnamed lambs were twins. They ate from their mother, but since she was short of milk, I supplemented their diet with a bottle. Squirt had his own bottle. I let the other two share the second bottle, until all three lambs' tummies bulged. "That'll keep you until tonight."

I finish the remaining chores of feeding, watering, and checking, scoop up the empty lamb-milk bottles, and head toward the house. Back inside, I clean up, while contemplating my options. Besides being messy and a ton of work, I know feeding lambs a large amount of milk twice a day is not very natural for them, and it sometimes results in health problems like bloat or Enterotoxemia, also called overeating disease. And I can forget going away from home for more than twelve hours at a time while I have bottle lambs. I cannot expect a friend to mix milk in my kitchen and feed lambs twice a day. It was an unusual year not to have bottle lambs, so for at least eight weeks per year, I am stuck. I started to think about buying a milk goat, and decided to call my neighbor who had several of those precocious animals.

"Tim, you still have that Nubian-cross doe for sale?"

"Yeh, I'd sell JaJa." Tim laughed. "Glad to hear you're coming around to the goat side."

Tim had told me earlier that the goat was bred to kid (have babies) the same time my ewes were scheduled to lamb.

"She's a good milker, right?"

"JaJa should be able to feed her kids as well a lamb or two."

"Perfect. What are you asking for her?"

JaJa turned out to be quite a character, very engaging and friendly to people. She weighed far less than my ewes but was soon top in the pecking order. Her persuasion? She bit the ewes' ears. Yep, that is how JaJa dominated the much larger sheep. When she approached the feed bunk, the waterer, or her desired resting place, the sheep moved out of her way like the sea parting for the Israelites.

A few days after I brought JaJa home, she kidded three healthy babies, very cute, but not ideal, considering I needed her to feed my bottle lambs.

By this time, the twin bottle lambs were eating plenty of hay, so Squirt was the only lamb left still needing a bottle. He was strong and ate with gusto while I stood at JaJa's side, but if I so much as looked the other direction, she butted him away. I solved that by haltering her and tying her to a post while the lamb was nursing. Again, when I stood at her side, no problem, but when I walked away, *bam!*, she would kick the little guy until he quit trying to nurse. By this time, I was feeling that I had simply traded one problem—messy kitchen, too much time spent making milk—for another problem, that of having to stand at JaJa's side while the lamb nursed.

Then I got to thinking I should give her an incentive to let the lamb nurse. I always fed JaJa a special treat of mixed grains when she nursed the lamb, so this time when I stepped back, and she butted the lamb, I took the grain pan away. When she stood quietly and allowed him to nurse, I put the grain back in front of her. It didn't take long for JaJa to learn her lesson. I could not have trained a sheep this way. Either a ewe will take an orphan, or she will not.

JaJa taught me other differences between sheep and goats. When I let the sheep and JaJa graze near my lawn, JaJa always looked for her food in the trees. Sheep prefer to eat grass and will forage in a tree or bush only when there is no grass. Goats, on the other hand, prefer to browse on leaves and small branches from trees and bushes.

Another difference is that a goat has little tolerance for pain, even minor pain, whereas sheep rarely complain. When it came time for annual vaccinations, I injected JaJa as I did my ewes and lambs. She let out a startling, human-like sound that made me think I had hit an artery, highly unlikely since I was giving subcutaneous (just under the skin) injections. I removed the needle, checked for blood and tried again. Same response. Finally, the third time, I completed the injection. When discussing this experience later with a goat producer, I learned JaJa's response was not unusual, and I had done nothing wrong in administering the vaccination.

JaJa was part of our operation for many years and fed

several orphan lambs to weaning age. When she did something puzzling that I later learned was normal goat behavior, it reminded me again of how different are goats and sheep. It also reminded me of Matthew 25:32-46, where Jesus separates the goats from the sheep in the final judgment. The sheep represent true believers, the righteous. The goats are symbolic for imposters, those who look like believers, but have no true faith or individual conviction. I find it interesting that, despite goats being more independent and considered smarter than sheep, in this parable sheep are the good guys.

In this context, the desirable characteristic of sheep is their compliant nature. While compliance is certainly not always a good trait, in our attitude toward the Good Shepherd it is very important, perhaps the most important characteristic a believer can possess. In this parable, a goat's independent self-reliance represents the unwillingness of people to humble themselves before the Lord and come to him on his terms, not theirs.

One last observation: The good things done by the sheep in this parable are not how their salvation is secured. The selfless acts noted are merely outward evidence of the condition of the believer's heart. The only way to truly please our Great Shepherd is to be wholly surrendered to him. When the will of the believer is surrendered to the Lord, good works will be the natural result. He sees good works for their own sake as hypocrisy.

–Marilyn

To Ponder:

- What is my motivation for the good things I do? Am I more interested in impressing others than doing what God wants me to do?
- Am I selective in what I surrender to the Good Shepherd?
- What do I need to do to be completely surrendered, and therefore useful to my Lord?

To Pray:

Search me, Good Shepherd, and clearly reveal any way I am not completely surrendered to you. Help me let go of these things and put them under your control and direction. I give you my life, and everything I think I control, for your service. Teach me to consider surrendering my will to the Good Shepherd the strongest and most courageous thing I can do.

13
Forgiven Sin and Wool

Come now, let us reason together," says the LORD. "Though your sins are like scarlet, they shall be as white as snow; though they are red as crimson, they shall be like wool.

–Isaiah 1:18 (NIV)

"Up and at 'em, boys." Dad always called his three daughters, 'boys.' It was part of his lighthearted approach to life. "We need to set up the barn before the shearers get here."

"Coming." Still drowsy with sleep, I sat on the edge of my bed and pulled on my rattiest jeans and an old, stained T-shirt.

The sun had just peaked over the eastern horizon when I joined my two younger sisters, Shelly and Marla, in the kitchen. We grabbed buttered toast that Mother had left for us, then went out to the barn. The April morning promised warmth. Even at that early hour, beads of perspiration gathered on my neck and face.

"Now that we're all here, let's run the ewes into the barn," Mom directed. She and Dad had already set up the temporary panel fencing to collect the sheep for shearing. "Spread out behind them and together we need to push them toward the gate . . . but not too hard. A master at moving sheep, Mom once again succeeded at directing her teenage and younger daughters in the art of transferring a skittish flock from one place to another.

The ewes settled in, and we moved on to the next task, setting up the wool bag. Dad directed us to fit three heavy metal legs into a thick metal ring three feet in circumference.

"Looks good, boys. Let's pick it up." The stand that would house the big wool bags weighed at least fifty pounds and stood twelve feet off the ground. "I've got this side. Marilyn, you're the tallest, so you can lift your end toward me." The stand teetered into place, with Dad steadying it. "Marla, bring me the wool bag. Shelly and Marilyn, you can bring the ladder over here." He pointed to a spot next to the wool bag stand.

Dad climbed the ladder, the coarse, itchy wool bag in tow. Just when he had finished securing a chain around the metal ring at the top of the bag to keep it in place, we heard the crunch of tires on gravel. The shearers had arrived.

"I get to do the wool bag," my youngest sister Marla shouted. "It's my turn."

"Sure, packing the wool is a good job for you. After about ten fleeces are in the bag, we'll help you down into it," said Mom, who then headed out of the barn to greet the shearers.

Shelly and I smiled at each other knowingly. We would have argued not to "do the wool bag." The person assigned to packing the wool stayed in the bag as new fleeces were thrown in, continuing to pack the wool until the bag was full. Because wool packing had been our jobs in previous years, Shelly and I could testify that jumping on the fluffy wool is great fun for the first five minutes. Then, the reality that this is real work sets in. It is not only hard work to jump and push the wool into open spaces, it is hot and smelly. Bits of hay, straw, and dirt stick to the packer's sweaty body and make their way between clothing and skin. It is a hot, stuffy, even claustrophobic job.

Shelly volunteered to carry the shorn fleeces up the ladder and drop them, one at a time, into the giant wool bag. I was sure she relished getting a firsthand look at Marla's angst when our younger sister was on fleece #50. Because I was oldest and biggest, I was assigned the job of catching and bringing sheep to the shearers. Good shearers remove a fleece every two to three minutes, making this a physically taxing job. No bathroom breaks.

Mom had hired these same two shearers in previous years. They entered the barn, lugging their electric shearers, cans of oil to lubricate the shearing blades, spare blades, sharpeners and electric extension cords. Neither man was big or notably muscular. Only as the shearing began did I appreciate their athleticism to lift and turn two-hundred pound sheep with one hand while wielding razor sharp, electric shearers in the other.

Within the first thirty minutes of shearing, the beads of sweat on my face and neck became streams of perspiration running down every part of my body. The constant work paused only when the shearers needed to change or sharpen their blades. We all savored a few minutes of rest before resuming the frenzied pace.

"Is it time for dinner?" Marla had taken up residence in the wool sack. The fun was over.

"No, it's only nine o'clock." Mom shouted over the buzz of the shearers. Other than a break to drink strong, unsweetened iced tea flavored with mint from her garden, we didn't rest until all the ewes and three rams were shorn—about one hundred fifty sheep in all.

It was nearly one o'clock when Mom, Shelly, Marla, the shearers and I finished and trudged into the house to eat. Dad, who had been doing other farm work, joined us for dinner. Farm and ranch families called the noon meal, the largest meal of the day, dinner.

Pot roast never tasted so good. Another year of shearing was over.

Now, as an adult in charge of my own flock, I oversee

shearing, which includes providing a hot meal fit for hungry laborers while directing the shearing in the barn. One of the first questions non-farmers ask when they learn I raise sheep is about shearing and selling wool. I explain to them that I hire a shearer. If I were to do the shearing myself, instead of two to three minutes per fleece, it would take twenty to thirty minutes per fleece, turning shearing into a week-long project.

People are always surprised to learn what I pay a shearer exceeds today's value of the wool. The price paid for wool when adjusted for inflation has dropped precipitously, especially for the wool from meat-breed sheep I raise. This wool is coarser and of less value than that of wool-breed sheep. When Mother was young, she could feed a ewe, even a meat breed, all year on the money she made from selling the ewe's fleece. Things have changed. For my operation, shearing is not a source of income but a task to check off the to-do list. Many people are surprised by this, since the retail price of wool garments is higher than garments made from other fibers.

Despite relatively low farm prices for this commodity today, wool has always had value. In Bible times, wool and linen (made from flax plants) were the only fibers people had. During U.S. colonial times, England tried to cripple economic development in the colonies by discouraging importation of breeding sheep, but colonists smuggled sheep into the New World and developed a thriving wool industry. During this time both boys and girls learned to spin and weave wool. Learning these skills was considered patriotic. England later outlawed colonial participation in the wool trade, which along with the Stamp Act, led to the Declaration of Independence and the Revolutionary War in 1776.

Fast forward to the early twentieth century where we

find the U.S. government enacting financial incentives to increase wool production for use in the construction of military uniforms.

Despite the historical importance of wool, when I read Isaiah 1:18 for the first time, I didn't understand why God likened forgiven sin to wool. The scripture does not say "as white as wool." In fact, raw wool is not bright white. It may look white against a green pasture, but it tends more toward a creamy hue. Here is this shepherd's take on why God compares forgiven sin to wool.

Few consumers consider that the beautiful wool garment or carpet they bought started as a coat worn by a sheep for a full year without being laundered. Sheep producers and those in the industry know wool must be shorn, sorted, washed, carded, dyed, and knitted or woven before it is made into something beautiful and useful. Just as a buyer doesn't think about what was required to get wool from a sheep's body to a fine wool jacket, we will never fully appreciate what it took to secure our salvation. I love that this Isaiah passage was written before Christ's sacrifice on the cross. God, because he is not confined by time and space, inspired the prophet Isaiah to write about a reality that was yet to come.

I also believe our Good Shepherd used wool as a symbol of forgiven sin because there is no fabric that is more durable. Isn't it comforting and warming to know God's forgiveness will never wear out or change?

Finally, wool fleeces when wet from rain or dew sparkle in the sunlight. They look as though they are encrusted with tiny crystals. Because God is pure and holy, and because he loves us, could it be that forgiven sin looks as beautiful to him as sparkling wool?

–*Marilyn*

To Ponder:

- What assurance do I have that my sin is forgiven and will never be counted against me?
- How would truly believing I am forgiven change my walk of faith?
- Does knowing I am completely forgiven change the way I view myself and others?

To Pray:

Shepherd of my soul, I cannot fully understand the depth of your sacrifice at Calvary, but I am so thankful you paid this price for me and every other human. I thank you that this sacrifice opens the door for me and that all I must do is to walk through the door. Let me live each day in the reality that I am fully forgiven. Thank you for the assurance (in Psalm 103:12) that you remove our sins from us "as far as the east is from the west."

14
That Pesky Process, Adversity

Consider it pure joy, my brothers and sisters, whenever you face trials of many kinds, because you know that the testing of your faith produces perseverance. Let perseverance finish its work so that you may be mature and complete, not lacking anything. . . . . Blessed is the one who perseveres under trial because, having stood the test, that person will receive the crown of life that the Lord has promised to those who love him.

–James 1: 2-4, 12 (NIV)

"**Mom, I've been thinking** that I'd like to buy some Southdown ewes to cross with my Suffolk ram." I had been in the sheep business as an adult for only a couple of years when I called my mom to ask her about my idea. "I really like how mild mannered and hearty Southdown-Suffolk offspring are, and they produce nice, big cuts of meat."

"Southdowns are easy to work with. I think that's a good direction." Mom always provided a trusted sounding board for my ideas.

"Do you know anyone who is raising purebred Southdowns?" Southdowns had lost much of their popularity back when I was a teenager. The show industry favored the larger, leaner Suffolk breed.

"I'll ask around and check the livestock papers." This was her specialty, finding the nail in a haystack.

A few weeks later, she called to tell me she had located a lady who wanted to sell three registered Southdown ewe lambs. *Perfect*, I thought.

"But, there is something you need to know about her.

When I called to ask about the ewe lambs she had for sale, well, by her talk I could tell she's a bit of an animal rightist."

"A what?" I worked in agricultural communications and had heard of people who believed animals and humans were equally valuable and had the same rights.

"She said you will have to be interviewed before she will allow you to purchase her sheep." Mom encouraged me to make an appointment to be "interviewed."

I did. Two days later, I followed directions to her address in the Colorado foothills west of Denver. Her place was small but tidy. Two adult ewes and three lambs grazed a small pasture close to the house. As soon as I pulled my pickup and trailer into the yard, a woman emerged from the house. I parked where directed, got out, and followed her to the small pasture. She showed me the three lambs she had for sale. Then the interview commenced.

I was straightforward. "I plan to breed the ewes to produce meat lambs or replacement ewes for my flock."

She seemed less than thrilled with this. "When do you wean your lambs?"

"I leave lambs on their mamas longer than most folks, usually about three months." I wondered if the deal was off.

"Do your sheep get to eat pasture?"

I really did want to buy the ewe lambs. They seemed healthy and looked well proportioned. "We have seventy acres of pasture, and I graze them as long as I have grass. In bad years, they eat mostly hay, but when we get rain, the sheep are on pasture most of the summer."

Apparently my answers pleased her, because she agreed to sell me the ewe lambs.

She asked what name to put as "owner" on the Southdown's registration papers then said, "I don't think I'll breed my ewes again."

"No? Why is that?" I was focused on making out my

check to pay for the three lambs.

"It was so much work. Two weeks before the lambs were due, I started sleeping outside in the barn."

Wow, I thought, *that is commitment*. "It's really cold in February."

"Yeah, and I didn't sleep so well." She sighed. "When the lambs were born, I took them in the house to clean and dry them off."

"How long did you have them in the house?" I have brought lambs on the edge of death into my house to keep them from dying, but I always get them back with their mothers as soon as they seem viable.

"Half a day."

"Did their mothers accept them when you returned them?"

It was clear this woman did not understand that as a ewe licks the afterbirth off her newborn lamb, it bonds as a unit with them. It is still not scientifically clear exactly what happens in this important process, but the ewe's special odor is transferred to the lamb, or the ewe absorbs the odor of the lamb as her own. It is not an odor humans can distinguish; but sheep can. Odor is the primary way ewes identify their lambs. If the odor is not right, the ewe will not permit the lamb to eat. A hungry lamb that is not getting enough from its own mother may try to nurse on other ewes; but once the ewe sniffs the lamb, she will butt it away.

She seemed puzzled by my question. "Yes, but later we lost the lambs that belonged to Pumpkin." She pointed at the smaller of the two ewes.

"So, the three lambs belong to the other ewe?" I was confused.

"No, we felt bad that Pumpkin couldn't raise a lamb, so we bought Spring from a breeder who isn't far from here." She brightened. "Spring was a triplet. The breeder said her mother wanted her but just didn't have enough milk to feed three lambs. Pumpkin took Spring, no problem."

We loaded the three friendly ewe lambs, the woman said a tearful goodbye, and I promised to let her know how her "babies" got along with my flock.

From the moment I released the three Southdown ewe lambs into my flock, I could tell that Spring, the adopted lamb, had more natural sheep instinct than the other two. She stayed with the rest of the flock and would shy away from anything that was new to her, such as our dog or the horses. The other two didn't quite act like sheep. When we let the flock out on pasture, we had to chase in these two separately. But, the big difference between the lambs' behaviors became evident when they gave birth the following year.

Spring had a little trouble birthing. I had to pull her huge ram lamb, but once it was on the ground, she incessantly talked to it and thoroughly licked it. She was instantly protective, shooing her lamb into the corner of the lambing jug when I came into the pen to check him and feed her. She became a very good mother to Buddy, who would go on to become grand champion breeding sheep at the county fair and later make an appearance at the National Western Stock Show in Denver.

A few weeks after Buddy was born, the second Southdown ewe gave birth. Fortunately, the lamb was strong enough that it had gotten up on its own, but none of its afterbirth had been removed by the ewe. When I found the pair, the mother was several feet away, looking at her lamb with curiosity. She didn't dislike him; she just seemed to lack any mothering instinct. This lamb was aggressive, anxious to have his first meal, so I was able to help him nurse. Eventually, the ewe accepted her lamb, but she was a neglectful mother. It didn't seem to matter one way or the other to the ewe if the lamb nursed or not. Sometimes, it takes new ewes a bit of time to learn to be good mothers, but this ewe never did.

About a week later, this ewe's twin sister gave birth to a set of twins. I found the final Southdown ewe's twin baby lambs dead and covered with afterbirth. Their mother was nowhere near them. Normally when a ewe loses a lamb, she calls and searches frantically for it for hours, even days, after it has died. But like her twin, this ewe didn't seem to have a care in the world.

Had this neglectfulness occurred once, I might have chalked it up to just one of those things you can't explain. But when both ewes exhibited the same, bizarre behavior, while their flockmate Spring had no mothering issues, I began to understand a sheep's mothering instinct is really more learned than instinctual. Research and conversations with other shepherds have confirmed this conclusion.

The lady who sold me these twins had done them (and me) no favors by cleaning them off in the warmth and comfort of her home. She had wanted to enhance their futures by cleaning them herself, but what she had done was to remove the "sheep sense" from them, particularly as it had to do with mothering babies. These ewes who had never been properly mothered, were unable to mother their offspring.

As many parents have learned, we do our children no favors by rescuing them from every difficult situation. We can support and encourage a child, or someone else, going through difficulties; but it may not be the best solution to remove them from the situation. Whether child or adult, we often learn best from life's failures and the challenges we must overcome to get back on our feet. This applies to learning life lessons as well as learning spiritual truths.

As James says, trials and testing produce perseverance,

and we must persevere to mature. Without maturity we cannot please God. Few of us like trials, but we can look forward to the end results, the character-building maturity, the crown of life that enduring of trials will bring us. There just aren't any effective ways to bypass trials and still mature.

–Marilyn

TO PONDER:

- In what ways might I be taking myself away from the discomfort God has designed to provide me growth and lead me into maturity?
- Am I helping my children or others out of adversity, rather than through it, thus depriving them of the opportunity to grow and mature?
- What is meant by the "crown of life" in this Scripture?
- Thinking about us as a society, how does our desire to avoid discomfort and difficulties ultimately hurt us?

TO PRAY:

Good Shepherd, develop my character. Let me grow up in you. If this means I must go through difficulties, let me learn and not complain. Help me grow and be able to help others as they go through trials. Most of all, I want to be pleasing to you. Do what you must to bring this about, and give me the grace to prosper through the difficulty.

15
Beware of Wolves

But when He saw the multitudes, He was moved with compassion for them, because they were weary and scattered, like sheep having no shepherd.

–Matthew 9:36 (NKJV)

As I drove the old pickup past a neighbor's field, I was not prepared for the sight that was spread before me. I blurted out, "What in the world happened! Oh, those poor babies."

The midwinter cold temps nipped at my face, telling me to stay inside. However, I wanted to look at the large flock of sheep grazing on our neighbor's cornstalks—just because I enjoy looking at sheep.

It was immediately apparent that something was not right. Lambs usually stay in bunches as they graze, but this time they were scattered across the large field and were aimlessly milling about. I parked my pickup and got out to see what was happening. Slowly I walked toward the nearest lambs. Normally they would have dashed away from me, but not this time. Some of them were bleeding from jagged rips in their skin; handfuls of wool dangled from their bodies. Those who were able to walk staggered toward me as though asking for help. This was a strange reaction, since they didn't know me; I was not their shepherd.

Spread throughout the field were many wounded and dying sheep, a sickening sight. Meanwile, other neighbors had arrived on the gruesome scene.

"Did coyotes do this?" "Whose dogs got in here?"

"Where was the herder?" "What happened?"

We learned that the hired shepherd had left his flock alone the night before. The shepherd of this flock had gone into town for a night of revelry and ended up in jail. His sheepdogs had apparently also taken the night off and were nowhere to be seen. In his absence, a group of renegade dogs had attacked the defenseless flock of lambs, ripping and tearing the flesh right off their bodies. The dogs devastated the lambs until they tired of the fun and returned to their homes. The lambs were terrified and confused. Many had suffered unbelievable pain. Their shepherd—their guardian—had left them alone to fend for themselves.

Surprisingly, most dogs that attack sheep are neither wild nor homeless. Many are beloved pets, and some are working dogs. But when two, three, or more get together, they can become vicious and destructive. One time when dogs entered our sheepfold, tearing up some of our ewes before they were discovered, I learned they were sheep dogs belonging to a sheepherder with a large flock of sheep that grazed winter cornstalks not far from our place. This sheepherder, also, had left his flock and dogs while he went into town to relieve his boredom. Sheepdogs are very high-energy animals and have to be busy doing something. They will find something to do on their own if the shepherd is not there to direct their activity, and often it is not a constructive endeavor. Guided and trained by a good sheepherder, they are beautiful to watch as they nimbly obey his commands. To a professional herder, one good sheepdog is worth more than several men.

As we travel through life, we are constantly attacked by sin in various ways. This is especially true if we have quit following our Shepherd, who wants only the best for us, his lambs. However, unlike the sheepherder in this story, our Shepherd will never abandon us. We are so vulnerable to temptation and easily tricked by the enemy when we let our guard down. Sin leaves us with horrible wounds and deceives us into thinking we are OK. When we try to function without our Shepherd, this is a perfect time for "the enemy" to get a foothold in our lives and lead us astray. It is so important to be fed spiritual food by a godly pastor who preaches from the Bible. I liken pastors to sheepdogs: they help care for the flock but get their guidance from the heavenly Shepherd. It is critical that we meet together with other Christians for protection from the "world" and we need to be led by a shepherd who follows the Lord.

There are times when we find ourselves slowly pulled into thoughts and actions that are not conducive to the Christlike life we aspire to live. We may become confused about decisions or problems and what actions we should choose. As a result we become weary and our thoughts are scattered. But Jesus will have compassion on us. We may have friends and acquaintances who can give us godly advice, but be careful. Unlike the shepherd in this story, our Shepherd Jesus has promised to never leave us or forsake us. His "sheepdogs" will be there to guard and protect us, but only if they follow his guidance and teachings. So, choose your earthly shepherds wisely!

–Millie

To Ponder:

- What things cause me to give up hope and become discouraged? How can I remove or disable these things that cause me to become disheartened?
- Do I have friends with whom I can confide my deepest thoughts and concerns? Will they pray with me?

- What would be the results if my heavenly Shepherd were to leave me alone and not be there to guide me?
- Do I have a godly "sheepdog," or friend, who will watch over me, rebuke me when needed, and be there for me? Am I willing to be that kind of friend to someone else?

TO PRAY:

Heavenly Father, thank you for being my Shepherd. You have promised to never leave me nor forsake me, and I thank You for that very comforting promise. Please be my protection when "wild dogs" come into my life with the intent of harming me. Show me the difference between the "wild dogs" and the "sheep dogs" that are there to guard and protect me. Lead me into fellowship with others whose source of guidance for their lives is your Word and your Holy Spirit.

Sheep, though defenseless, are protective of their babies.

16
The Perfect Substitute

Who Himself bore our sins in His own body on the tree, that we, having died to sins, might live for righteousness—by whose stripes you were healed. For you were like sheep going astray, but have now returned to the Shepherd and Overseer of your souls.

–I Peter 2:24-25 (NKJV)

"Is it OK if we go out and ride the calves, Mom? We have all our chores done," queried our oldest daughter. It was a lovely calf-riding morning on the Bay farm and the three daughters didn't want to waste any opportunity on such a day.

"Yes, but don't let Netta ride a calf. I don't want her to get hurt, and I don't think her folks would approve."

When our girls were young, we purchased our farm, believing it would be a wonderful place to raise our kids. The passing years confirmed that this momentous decision had been the right one. The three girls had chores to do and kept very busy, but they also had time, after they finished their work, for fun.

Some of that fun involved the four baby calves we bought to eventually provide both meat for our freezer and some to sell. Feeding the young black and white babies with bottles gave the girls extra opportunity to learn responsibility.

As the furry little calves grew, our girls decided it would be a challenge to ride them, just like they had watched cowboys ride bulls at the rodeo. Occasionally their younger cousin from the city came to visit for a few days. Netta loved the farm and all the animals that came with it—horses, chickens, rabbits, sheep, kittens, puppies, and of course, the calves. Wide-eyed she watched her "big" cousins mount the black and white calves, hanging on for dear life as the creatures bucked and kicked around the corral. We were thankful the girls never received serious injuries, though they inevitably were dumped on the ground.

Feeling left out, Netta begged, "Please let Netta ride, too. Netta wants to do it."

She was just too young and we couldn't take the chance of her being injured; we weren't about to give in to her continued pleading.

Finally, though, light donned! Why not capture a sheep for Netta to ride? With a much shorter distance to fall, she wouldn't likely get hurt. Thus began the saga of Sally the "sheep-pony."

After coaxing a large, fairly gentle ewe into the barn, we prepared her for riding. First, we placed a halter with a lead rope on her head. Next came a tiny saddle which we had purchased for our small pony years before. Carefully placing Netta on the saddle, we instructed, "Hang on to the saddle horn." Then, to avoid any surprises, we led Sally around the corral. Much to our surprise, Sally did not buck or try to dislodge her diminutive rider. She carefully carried her load as though she had given rides many times.

"See, Netta can ride," she joyfully exclaimed. Netta lost the desire to ride the "cow" after that. She had her own "pony."

In the fall we attended a small fair where our girls exhibited their lambs. We took Netta with us to the fair, and after the sheep show, there was a small-town parade. Since we had planned to let Netta ride Sally in the parade, we had brought all the riding paraphernalia. The parade began, and here came Netta riding her "sheep-pony." We again led Sally, but that was OK with Netta. She might as well have been riding a beautiful, golden stallion; she was so proud of her steed. How the parade watchers smiled and clapped as she rode by.

Decades later, Netta and my daughters still reminisce about Sally and the fun she provided all of us. We even have a reminder, a photograph of Netta mounted on Sally holding the "reins" of her mighty steed and seated on a perfect, albeit tiny, Western saddle.

Sometimes substitutes result in superior outcomes. When I think of substitutes, I am always reminded of the greatest "switch" that ever happened. During creation, God made everything perfect, but that concept was destroyed when Adam and Eve committed the first sin in the Garden of Eden by disobeying God's command to not eat the fruit of the "tree of good and evil." Since that time, every baby is born with a sin nature. As a result, every human deserves death for his or her sin. But God provided a substitute to take our punishment. God sent his only Son, perfect Jesus, to earth to live as a man. Jesus suffered every temptation known to humanity, but he never weakened. He was totally without sin. Had he ever broken and sinned, he could not have been the substitute for our sin. When he died on the cross, he bore all our sins, an unimaginable weight. Jesus could have backed out of his commitment, but he willingly went through extreme torture and death on the cross. Why? Because of his incomprehensible love for us, a love which neither you nor I can perceive. He chose to be our substitute, a perfect substitute. He was willing to take our punishment. How can we not love him?

–Millie

TO PONDER:

• What would this world be like if Jesus had not willingly taken my punishment?

• How would/do people live if there is no hope for eternity with him? How might I reach out to people in the world who have no hope—even those in my own community?

• What are some ways I can share this glorious hope with others close to me?

• Have I fully accepted the fact that Jesus was my substitute when he died on the cross?

TO PRAY:

Heavenly Shepherd, thank you for providing your Son to be my substitute. I can't even comprehend the extreme punishment I deserve, yet Jesus took my place on the cross. I can't envision how you could love me so much, either! Please help me when I am tempted to do something that is not pleasing to you. Help me to remember, Jesus, how much you love me—so much that you gave your life for me.

17
Whose Brand Do You Wear?

For every beast of the forest is Mine, and the cattle on a thousand hills.

–Psalm 50:10 (NKJV)

"Hey, that's my cow! You're stealing my cattle." Angry voices cried as the cattle were rounded up and sorted.

"You can't prove which ones are yours; I think they're *mine.* And anyway, they're mine now!" came the defiant answer.

In the "old days" this type of scene often played out, sometimes with such anger that a gun fight ensued, and one or more cowboys ended up dead. Thankfully, when various ways of identifying cattle, horses, and sheep came into use, many such angry and deadly scenes were avoided.

Nowadays, in most cattle and sheep operations, the animals are identified with a "brand." Cattle are branded with either a hot iron or a liquid mixture that is extremely cold (sometimes dry ice and alcohol). This method is called "freeze branding." Either method leaves a visible mark identifying the owner.

"But doesn't branding hurt the animal?" you ask.

"Sure, but not very long, and it's not extremely painful; not a lot more than when you get an injection for measles or mumps. And the calves seem to forget about it right away as they return to grazing or playing with the other babies; the momentary scary experience passes quickly."

Sheep, on the other hand, may be marked in special wool paint with their owner's identifying brand. Or, both sheep and cattle may be identified with notches clipped in the animals' ears in a certain pattern. Both may have tags fastened in each animal's ear. The downfall of tags is the probability that they'll catch on brush or a fence and fall out.

Most owners of a herd of cattle or a flock of sheep have registered their identifying marks with the agriculture office in their state. This allows the rightful owners to claim their property. In many regions, several owners may pasture their cattle or sheep together in the same area. It is imperative to have a system to separate their animals when it is time to move them home, to gather up the young for weaning, tagging, docking, vaccinating, etc.

I was reminded one day, as we worked the lambs, of the importance of the identifying marks. My daughter Shelly and I were banding, vaccinating, and doing health checks on the lambs when I said, "Hey Shelly, have you seen a stray lamb? I'm sure #42 had twins but she only has one lamb with her now. They both had #42 painted on their left sides."

From the far side of the corral I heard, "#42 is clear over here, but he sure looks hungry. I think he has forgotten who his mother is. We'd better put her in a jug with both her lambs so they can get re-acquainted and make sure the ewe has plenty of milk for both."

I was thankful for the brand which can be read at a distance to match up mother and babies. This is especially important when a ewe has two or three lambs. It makes it much easier for the shepherd to notice whether or not all the lambs are getting enough to eat. Sometimes, in huge flocks of sheep when twins are born, the shepherd will tie a front leg of each lamb to a front leg of its twin to make sure the mother remembers she has two lambs. This method also keeps a lamb from wandering off from its mother. When both lambs are securely bonded to their mother, the rope is removed. Usually lambs become strong enough to bond and become somewhat independent after two or three days.

Years ago I owned a set of paint-branding "irons." At lambing time I faithfully branded the number on each ewe and her lamb(s) as they were born. (The ewes have to be branded annually because the wool is shorn off each year.) Since my flock was not as huge as the mega ranches of sheep, I decided to ear tag my ewes instead. Whatever the method of identification, keeping records enabled me to identify each ewe when she lambed. The lambs were tagged at birth, along with the necessary "minor surgeries" of docking tails (cutting them shorter) and neutering the little boy lambs.

Many people think docking is a barbaric practice, but it promotes a much healthier and cleaner lamb than if it was not done. Corrals are prone to bacteria and if the lambs' tails remain long, they can be infiltrated with all kinds of parasites and disease. Flies will lay their eggs on these filthy, manure-covered appendages, enabling the maggots to penetrate a lamb's body. It is not a pretty sight! Taking care of the problem is much more difficult than preventing it by docking the lambs' tails.

When we become a child of the King, we wear his brand. There are many ways we can be identified as a lamb of his flock. Inevitably he will need to do "minor surgeries" on us to keep us healthy, and some of these processes may be painful and difficult. But each "surgery" helps us grow closer to him and helps defray the evil one's attempts to take over our bodies. If only we could prevent these "maggots" from entering our lives and destroying the health of our souls.

We live in a huge universe with people of varying lifestyles, but if we belong to the Lord, our "brand" should be visible enough to set us apart so others know who our Shepherd is. How important it is to have someone else to whom we can relate. Like the twins whose feet are tied together, we need someone with whom we can bond and receive nourishment at the same time.

Do I get excited about wearing the Lord's "brand" or do I refuse to wear it where it will show, because it might make me feel uncomfortable? If I am to visibly wear his "brand," am I willing to wear the one he designs, or do I alter it so it fits my circumstances? After all, I am a child of the King, and no other brand could be more desirable! My Father owns the cattle on a thousand hills, and his brand is legal proof. If I do not wear my Shepherd's brand, then my brand must belong to the devil, and *that* I surely don't want!

–Millie

TO PONDER:

- Do you wear the brand of the Good Shepherd? Is it comfortable for you?
- How do we receive the brand of the Good Shepherd?
- When the lambs are sorted in the "end times" will the Good Shepherd claim you as one who wears his brand? Consider the consequences after "the sorting."
- Do you have a close friend with whom you can bond, share, and grow as you feed on God's Word?

TO PRAY:

Awesome Shepherd, thank you for the gift and privilege of wearing your brand. Help me to be a loving member of your flock. I am thrilled to be able to look to you for my protection, nourishment, and care. Assist me in learning as you discipline me. Give me patience and acceptance as you cleanse me from the maggots of sin. Enable my special friends to grow with me as we bond and learn together.

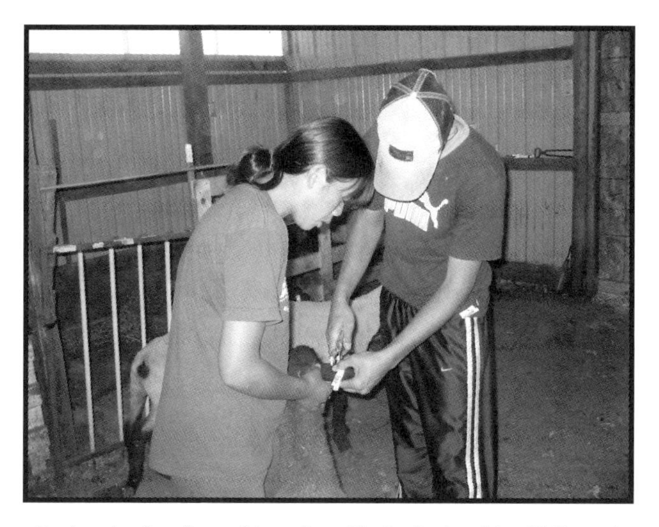

Ear tagging is a form of branding. Marilyn's daughter, Kelly, and Costa Rican friend, Diego, insert an ear tag.

The English restricted colonists from raising sheep and manufacturing wool. That action contributed to the American Revolution.

18
The Good Shepherd's Staff

Even though I walk through the darkest valley, I will fear no evil, for you are with me; your rod and your staff, they comfort me.

–Psalm 23:4 (NIV)

"Oh, Mom, that's disgusting." My daughter Kelly turned up her nose. "Won't it heal by itself?"

I paused in my examination of a big Suffolk ewe to answer. I looked up at Kelly; then I turned back to the boil-like lump the size of a large marble that protruded from the ewe's cheek. "No, I don't think it will heal itself."

I had noticed for the past week that this ewe wasn't eating normally. She would come to the feeder, nibble, then step back. She kept to herself while the other sheep nosed around looking for stems of hay or the occasional green weed.

"I need to lance it. Please get the scalpel and disinfecting spray."

Kelly returned with the requested items. "Here." She thrust them toward me and grabbed the crook that hangs on a hook by the gate.

My daughter walked up behind the ewe, hooked her neck in the crook, and pulled her head upwards. She dropped the crook and stood with the ewe's head cradled in her arms. "I'm ready, Mom."

"Can you give me some room?" I positioned myself on the same side of the ewe as Kelly. "I want to approach it from the opposite side, just in case she jumps and I can't control the scalpel."

Kelly nodded.

I made a quick cut at the bottom of the lump, and light green, hard pus began to ooze out.

"That's revolting." My daughter kept a tight hold on the ewe's head but turned her own head away.

"You're right, but think about how much better this poor ole gal will feel." I stroked the ewe's head before draining the wound and liberally applying disinfectant in and around it. "That should do it. You can let her go now. Thank you, Kelly. I know it wasn't a fun job, so I really appreciate your help today."

"Sure, Mom." Kelly is compliant and loves animals, but I didn't blame her for darting away from the barn as soon as we finished doctoring the ewe. I remained in the barn to put out hay for the evening feeding. I used a pitchfork to dislodge several flakes above my head and send them tumbling to the ground. I folded the flake of green, leafy alfalfa hay in half and scooped it up to carry it inside the barn. As I did, I contemplated Psalm 23 and chuckled to myself that this ewe probably didn't feel comforted when my daughter captured her with our crook. Also known as a staff, this is an important tool for the shepherd to use in managing a flock.

To King David, the Lord's rod and staff were a comfort. Sheep flocks in biblical times depended on large expanses of common grazing land. The shepherd had the responsibility of daily leading his flock to green pastures and clear waters. Today, in many parts of the world, shepherding has changed little. These shepherds are skilled and trained men, whose full-time job is to find good grass for their flocks and to protect their sheep from predators—both animal and human. They take the flocks back to a protected paddock at night, or they create a makeshift structure within the common grazing area. These shepherds are not only knowledgeable of the sheep and their nutritional needs, they also spot injured and sick animals and know how to treat them. They are strong and can take down a predator. The rod referred to in Psalm 23:4 was a weapon that could be used to throw at or club a predator.

In contrast to this type of shepherding, my mother's and my sheep operations are called farm flocks. We may graze our animals, but the pastures are typically fenced and do not depend on my constant presence. Rather than a rod, I have a rifle at the ready to ward off coyotes or stray dogs that threaten my sheep. Farm flock shepherds do, however, make good use of a crook or staff. While the shepherds in David's day likely fashioned their own staffs, I choose mine from a sheep supply catalog called Premier. This supplier has researched the products it offers, and buyers can choose from an array of different sizes and elastic properties. This supplier offers head catch or leg catch staffs. The staff I chose catches the heads of my fairly large Suffolk and Southdown ewes. I passed on the leg catch staff, because I fear I will hurt a ewe by catching it that way, and because a sheep's kick can give a hard rattle to the shepherd's arm. My staff is not strong enough, nor would I be able to hold the straight part of it, if I were to hook the three-hundred pound ram's head in the staff loop. To catch big rams, I resort to a lariat; but for multiple catches within a flock of ewes, I use my dependable staff.

Both the rod and the staff are for the sheep's benefit. The rod is both aggressive and defensive. It is used to keep danger away from the flock. Like the smooth, light metal and gentle curve of my crook, the staff is more of a nurturing instrument. Traditionally, a staff was used to pull a lamb or ewe out of a dangerous place.

In today's farm flocks, the staff is used to pull one animal out of a flock with as little trauma as possible. I often use my staff to pull out a lamb or ewe for routine medical treatments, as well as to examine animals when I suspect they may have health problems that need attention, such as this ewe with the lump on her mouth. Except for right after shearing, a sheep's thick wool disguises problems, such as cysts, cuts, or malnutrition. If a shepherd suspects a problem, much as I did when I saw that the ewe wasn't eating normally, he must catch the sheep to examine and treat it. This often involves the shepherd working his hands over the sheep's entire body and parts the wool until he finds the problem. Neither the detection of an ailment nor its treatment is enjoyable, but it is necessary for the welfare of the sheep.

Just as a sheep doesn't enjoy the shepherd's probing, I am often uncomfortable with my Good Shepherd's examination of me, especially if I am trying to hide something from him. How truly ridiculous to think I can hide a single thing from him; he knows it is there before I do.

Not long ago, I was praying about what I believed to be a stronghold in the life of a family member. I paused to ask the Lord if there was something in my life that he wanted me to change in order to have this stronghold removed in my family member's life. He revealed with abrupt clarity that a particular television program on the History Channel was creating a problem in my home. I grabbed my remote and deleted all past and future recordings of this program. Earlier in my walk with him, I would have ignored or denied this revelation, but I am learning that I will have no peace until I yield to God's direction in my life. I don't want to infer that this program was wrong for someone else to watch. However, because I allowed the Lord to examine me closely, he revealed that for me, at that time, the program's portrayal of pagan religious practices was interfering with the removal of someone else's stronghold.

Just as I feel hesitation and distaste when doctoring a sheep, I know the Good Shepherd feels my pain through the doctoring and recovery process. I force doctoring on my sheep because it will benefit them. But our Lord will not force spiritual healing on us. He waits for our willingness.

–Marilyn

TO PONDER:

- Am I keeping the Good Shepherd at arm's length because I don't want him to see my wounds? My sin?
- Have I considered that it would be much better to go through the short-term pain to start healing and foster further growth in my spiritual life than to continue to suffer from something my Lord wants to change or remove?

TO PRAY:

Healing Shepherd, give me the courage to let you examine me for wounds, as well as for any hidden sin that displeases you and makes me less useful to your purposes. Let me submit to your healing balm, even though it may be painful and awkward. Through the process of this examination and treatment, help me draw closer to you.

19
Get In The House!

Then Moses summoned all the elders of Israel and said to them, "Go at once and select the animals for your families and slaughter the Passover lamb. Take a bunch of hyssop, dip it into the blood in the basin and put some of the blood on the top and on both sides of the door frame. None of you shall go out of the door of your house until morning. When the Lord goes through the land to strike down the Egyptians, he will see the blood on the top and sides of the door frame and will pass over that doorway, and he will not permit the destroyer to enter your houses and strike you down.

–Exodus 12:21-23 (NIV)

On a brisk fall Sunday afternoon the phone rang. "Hi, Marilyn. Chris has got some cattle out. Any chance you might be able to help us get 'em back into his corral?" It was my friend Angie. She and my neighbor Chris were cattle people.

"Sure, do you want me on foot or horseback?"

"Horseback would be good. When can you be there?"

"Should take me about thirty minutes to saddle up and ride over to Chris's place." I didn't often get to chase cattle horseback. "Should I leave now?"

"As soon as you can. We're headed out as soon as I get off the phone."

I pulled on a hooded sweatshirt and my heavy chore coat. I grabbed my winter work gloves then rushed out the door. The cold wind whipped my face.

At the corral I haltered my trusty sorrel mare, Lady, and

led her to the hitching post. I ran a brush over her body to remove burs or other debris to prevent them from irritating her when I snugged up the saddle. Once saddled and bridled, I mounted and directed Lady toward my neighbor Chris's place. It was a little over a mile away.

Ten minutes later, I reached the end of Chris's lane. He, Angie, and Angie's husband were trying to push a wild-looking black heifer toward the open corral gate, but she would have none of it. When they got close to her, instead of moving away from them toward the gate, she would bolt past them and run down the pasture fence line.

Lady and I hung back, so that when the heifer bolted toward the fence line, we were there to dissuade her. Even with a fast, agile horse blocking her escape, the heifer refused to go through the open corral gate. Finally, the men had to take out a panel in the pasture fence, so that the heifer could rejoin the other cattle through a gate on the opposite side of the corral. Even then, she tried several times to break and run in the wrong direction.

We all let out whoops and hollers when the ornery heifer finally ran through the opening, and Chris slammed the gate behind her.

"Let me say how very glad I am to be a sheep gal." I couldn't resist the opportunity to jibe the panting cattlemen. "It took four intelligent stock handlers over an hour to get one bad-tempered heifer back into the corral. All I have to do if my sheep get out is call them, and the entire flock comes running home!"

They took my teasing in good humor. On my ride back home I thought more about the nature of sheep compared to cattle and other animals.

Sheep are skittish and require very little persuasion to run back home to the sheep pen. I believe God made them this way because they are virtually defenseless. They can outrun a person but not a predator. Their teeth are made for grinding grass, not fighting off an attacker. And, while they will kick if their leg is held up, they would never aggressively kick an attacker. Because of their vulnerability, sheep are very sensitive to danger. With one glance, even at a distance, the shepherd can tell if his flock is feeling threatened.

As I pondered this, I was reminded of one day not long ago when I watched my neighbor's Toy Poodle cut across the back of my pasture. The next thing I knew, my entire flock of thirty ewes was high tailing it to the barn. Another time, I saw the ewes crowding into the loafing shed, an extension of the barn with one side open. Then I caught a glimpse of a coyote darting from behind the haystack on the far side of the sheep pen. The coyote was not in the pen and likely could not have gotten in, but the sheep were on high alert and crowded into where they felt safest, where they could take cover from the danger. This is not such a bad lesson for us.

When the Israelites were enslaved in Egypt, God used Moses to bring ten successive plagues on the Egyptians. The goal of the plagues was to persuade Pharaoh to release the Israelites from Egyptian slavery. God used the plagues to specifically undermine the Egyptians' confidence in their gods. According to Exodus 11:9, Pharaoh's unwillingness to release the Israelites after the first nine plagues was so that "My wonders may be multiplied in the land of Egypt."

The final plague finally convinced Pharoah, and he finally let the Israelites leave Egypt. But this plague's implications extend far beyond this historic event. To this day, the descendants of the Israelite slaves who were released celebrate this event as Passover in the Jewish calendar's first month of the year.

In anticipation of the tenth and final plague, each family was commanded to bring a lamb into its house on the tenth day of the month. On the fourteenth day of the same month, the family was commanded to kill this lamb at twilight and to smear the blood on the top and sides of the door frame. Then, all members of the family and the neighboring family, if they were sharing a lamb, were to eat the meat. They were also commanded to stay inside the house all night.

The following morning when they awoke to hear the lamenting of their Egyptian neighbors, the Israelites must have been exceedingly glad they had followed God's instructions.

That night God had passed over the land, killing the firstborn of every person and animal that was not in a house with lamb's blood on the door frame. It took the loss of Pharaoh's own son for him to finally relent and release the Israelites from their bondage.

I lived in Taiwan for five years and was dumbstruck to learn that part of the Chinese New Year celebration is the posting of red paper on the top and sides of door frames. On the paper is written wishes for protection, good health, and prosperity. I don't think it is a coincidence that the Chinese do with paper what the Hebrews did with the Passover lamb's blood.

Again, the humble sheep has it right. At the slightest provocation, sheep run to the house (barn) for protection. During the tenth plague of Egypt, those who stayed in the houses with the lamb's blood on the top and side door frames were saved. Today, Jesus, the slain Lamb of God is the blood covering for our salvation and protection, but I must decide to place myself under his blood covering.

Get in the house!

–Marilyn

To Ponder:

- How can I have assurance that I am saved by Jesus' sacrifice?
- Meditate on the fascinating fact that God foretold his plan of salvation through Jesus' sacrifice centuries before it took place, by saving people covered by the blood of lambs in the tenth plague of Egypt.
- For a captivating study, research the plagues described in Exodus chapters 7-12, and how each of them undermined the power of an Egyptian god or an Egyptian religious belief.

To Pray:

Thank you, almighty and all-powerful God, that your provision for salvation and plan for reconciliation with humankind has been revealed to us clearly from the beginning of time. Thank you for this powerful story that shows me how you love me and have a plan for my life. Help me in times of danger to run into your protective fold.

A contented mama cares for her brood.

Blue has been a good, hardy, producing ewe.

20
The Little Ewe Who Thought She Could

But everyone who hears these words of mine and does not put them into practice is like a foolish man who built his house on sand. The rain came down, the streams rose, and the winds blew and beat against that house, and it fell with a great crash.

–Mathew 7:26-27 (NIV)

Lightning hopped across the sky in cadence with accompanying thunder as I made a dash for the field. *I've got to get those sheep in. Mike is coming to shear them tomorrow, and their wool needs to be dry.*

By the time I reached the pasture, most of the ewes had already darted home to the safety of the barn—all of them except Lilan, that is. She nonchalantly continued to graze, nipping each blade of grass as though she was analyzing the content. She looked up when I hollered, "Lilan, get in the barn; a storm is coming!" By then she was the lone sheep in the pasture, but she didn't care. There were other things on her mind. She waited for me to approach her before she hinted that she would come in to the barn.

Lilan was a diminutive specimen of a sheep. Her small, boxy body was supported by four, short black legs. Her face and ears were also black. Her mother was a Southdown, a small breed of sheep with tan face and legs, and her father was a Suffolk, a very large breed of sheep with black head and legs. Lilan sported the Suffolk face but it was set on a Southdown body. Personality-wise, she was more like a pussy cat. Anyone could walk right up to her anywhere in the corral or pasture to pet her or to visit with her.

However, that all changed the day she gave birth to twin lambs. When Lilan finally returned to the safety of the corral, we discovered her cleaning off two newborn babies. As was our routine, we set about moving the little family into a jug in the lambing barn where we could observe them and make sure all was well.

My husband, Marvin, easily picked up both lambs. Immediately, Lilan's other personality sprang into action. Trying to protect her babies, she began viciously, with all her strength, butting Marvin's legs. We stood there and laughed at the comical sight. Each time she butted him, her hind legs flew up in the air. She was so tiny that her butting did not faze Marvin, who is over six feet tall. Lilan's confidence never wavered; she attacked him again and again while we moved the little family to the barn.

Finally, with Lilan and her twins safely bedded down in the jug we fastened the gate. It was a cold winter day, so I climbed up one rung on the side panel of the pen to plug in a heat lamp. The newborn wet babies needed the heat lamp to dry off and warm up. As I stood up on the panel I felt something pinching my leg.

"Lilan, you bit me!" I shouted, shocked at the thought. Sheep don't bite, but Lilan certainly did that day as she used every defense she could think of. After a few days, she settled down to her amiable personality, and we were friends again.

That little ewe was full of confidence which was, in reality, a false confidence. She really was helpless in her defense against two large humans who, had we been so disposed, could have done her and her lambs a great deal of harm. But she never relented in her self assurance.

Similarly, Christians sometimes try to impress others by appearing to have all the answers. We *know* what churches or organizations are good and which are not. We *know* what activities will cause someone to fall from grace with God. We *know* what actions others should be taking in their everyday life. And of course, we *know* who will make it to Heaven or not, and why. The pretentious list goes on and on.

Ultimately, God alone knows the answers. The Bible tells us we only need to accept his Son, Jesus as our personal Savior who died in our place to cover our sins. It doesn't say we have to give up this or give up that, do this or do that. We need a genuine, confident faith in God. We need to settle it that he has provided for the forgiveness and cleansing of sin. We don't want to have false confidence, like little Lilan, that we can handle things our way. We must rely upon our heavenly Shepherd rather than trust in ourselves. Remember, the enemy is always lurking, waiting for an opportunity to attack our minds when we least expect it. Placing our confidence only in ourselves provides a perfect opportunity for the enemy to demoralize and discourage us.

The above passage of Scripture reminds me not to be like the foolish man. When he built his house on the sand, he probably didn't have a blueprint. He was trying to build a nice home where he could live and be comfortable, but because of his foolishness, his home was quickly destroyed. He took shortcuts in his project. Perhaps he was over-confident, lazy, or trying to save time and money. In true confidence we need to "build our house" on the rock, Jesus Christ. Then it will have a strong foundation, be sturdy and able to withstand the forces of evil which will surely attack us. If we don't follow God's blueprint for our "home," or life, the devil will ferociously butt us and bite us as he tries to take us down.

Sturdy and dependable tools are also a necessity. We can acquire these by getting involved in solid, Bible-based churches and/or Bible studies which teach and encourage our Christian values and morals. It is imperative that we seek out godly Christian leaders who teach from the Word of God. We must have a strong foundation if our "house" is to withstand all the forces of evil that will come our way.

–Millie

To Ponder:

- What are some ways I can have a genuine confidence in the course of my thoughts and activities?
- Do I ever have false confidence?
- What steps need to be taken to build my spiritual "house" on a solid foundation?
- Consider times when self confidence is a positive attribute.

To Pray:

Dear Father, thank you for being my heavenly Shepherd and for guiding me in everything I do. Forgive me for the times I have acted in false confidence and have forgotten to trust you. Help me to always look to you for help. Thank you for the privilege of building my life on your foundation.

21
Keep Out the Thief

The thief does not come except to steal, and to kill, and to destroy. I have come that they may have life, and that they may have it more abundantly.

–John 10:10 (NKJV)

Even in early June, perspiration dotted my face as I scrubbed carrots for supper. The phone rang. I hastily dried my hands and snatched up the phone before the call went to voicemail.

"Hello." The caller introduced herself as a neighbor I had met the previous summer. "I know you raise sheep. Are you missing any?" Two sheep had wandered into her yard earlier in the day, she said.

"What do they look like?"

When she seemed surprised by the question, I added, "What color are their faces? Are they shorn or wooled? How big are they?"

After some prompting, my neighbor, who was new to farm country, described the two sheep. "They are about the size of our Labrador Retriever, maybe a little shorter. They have light brown faces."

"Sounds like they are Southdowns."

"South what?"

I explained that Southdown sheep are an old English breed. They are small and stocky with light tan noses and more wool on their heads and legs than most breeds.

"Oh."

I had lost her with all the details. "I have several Southdown ewes in my flock. As far as I know, they are still in my pasture. But I will check."

I thanked her for calling, then hung up the phone. I slipped on my chore boots and walked out to the pen, curious to know whose sheep had shown up in my neighbor's yard. My own sheep were resting in the shade of our barn. A quick count revealed that all the Southdown ewes were accounted for. I called back the neighbor to let her know that the two mystery sheep weren't mine.

Next day, when I went out to do my morning feeding, I found a very bedraggled, skinny Southdown yearling ewe lying outside my sheep pen. What had happened to this poor baby?

As I approached the ewe, she stood up on unsteady legs. Injury, sickness, or inadequate nutrition had left her weak. I easily haltered the ewe and put her in a pen with plenty of leafy green alfalfa hay and water.

After feeding my own animals, I returned to the house and phoned my neighbor. "Have the sheep you called about yesterday left your house?"

"No, they are still here. I gave them hay and water. Is that OK?"

"Yes, that's good." I was in a hurry and decided not to explain how very strange it was that these sheep would separate from their flock and not return home. "A yearling ewe like the ones you described showed up here this morning. I'll call around and see whose sheep they are."

I immediately dialed my neighbor to the north. Sarah is a young woman, the mother of three boys, and a knowledgeable and resourceful shepherd. When she answered, I asked if she knew of anyone who was missing some Southdown ewes.

"They are probably mine."

"These ewes are sick and emaciated." I couldn't imagine

Sarah allowing her sheep to be in such bad health.

"Oh, Marilyn, I've never had to deal with a more devastating situation." Her voice quavered. "Last month a pack of fighting pit bulls broke into my pen at night. By the time I woke up, got my gun and ran out to the pen, the dogs had maimed or killed more than half the Southdowns."

"I had no idea. Whose dogs were they?"

"When we asked around, we learned that the pack of dogs had been trained to fight. The owners let them roam the countryside by night when no one would see and report them."

Now, any shepherd who has lost animals to predators knows that rogue dogs are the worst threat to vulnerable livestock. Coyotes are a threat to sheep, but they only kill to supply themselves and their pups with food. Rogue dogs, on the other hand, usually kill for recreation, and packs of dogs heighten the frenzy.

"There was blood and innards everywhere, even on the rafters of the barn." Sarah had gotten off a shot, but in the dark she was unable to hit anything. The shot only chased away the dogs. "My dad tried to run them down, but he couldn't track them in the dark."

The bloody carnage left by the pack of pit bulls was emotionally and financially devastating. Few of the sheep escaped unscathed. The dogs killed about a dozen, and another dozen had to be put down immediately. Sarah attempted to nurse the balance of the flock back to health. A number of the sheep disappeared that night, and she didn't know until I called her that some of them had survived. In the years that followed, Sarah continued to raise sheep but never was able to develop a flock of Southdown sheep as nice as those she had prior to the attack of the pit bulls.

Sarah's sad story made me think of Jesus' comments to his disciples that the thief (Satan) wants to destroy us, but Jesus wants to give us abundant life. Unlike Sarah's Southdown sheep that were savagely attacked, though, we have a choice of allowing or not allowing predators into our "sheep pen." Satan is adept at making believers think they are missing out on the fun. There is no doubt that sin can be alluring for a time, but the ultimate result is always devastation.

When Sarah described the destruction caused by the pit bulls, I remember thinking if only the dog owners could see what their fight-trained animals had done to those helpless sheep. But, when the authorities followed the blood trail to the house where the pit bulls lived, the residents had already vacated. How like the thief described in John 10:10 was this pack of dogs. The pit bulls destroyed this flock of sheep, and the dog owners bore no consequence for the crime. Instead, my neighbor had to bear the expense alone. Satan can be just like this. He beckons us to "come have fun" with him, but we alone will pay for the consequences of our sin.

From a distant vantage point, life over death and abundance over destruction are easy choices, but in the moment of temptation, the choice is not always as clear. I struggle with gluttony. (Even overeating sounds better than this "g" word. Yikes!) I don't want to be controlled by anyone or anything other than the Holy Spirit, so keeping my favorite ice cream in the freezer is one way I let the thief into my "sheepfold."

Satan is watching for opportunities to kill, steal, and destroy. The best time to choose life and abundance is now, before temptation comes.

–Marilyn

To Ponder:

- Is there any part of my life in which I am allowing the thief to steal, kill, or destroy?
- Am I living life to the full, as Jesus my Good Shepherd would want me to live?
- What changes can I make today to move me closer to the goal of living life abundantly?

To Pray:

Loving Shepherd, I ask you to close and seal the sheepfold around me, so that the thief cannot steal my joy or wreak havoc in my life. Search me today and show me any way that I am leaving holes in the sheepfold through which the thief can lure me to look beyond Jesus for my fulfillment.

A sheepdog named Woody, working sheep

22
Always With Me

Fear not, for I am with you. Be not dismayed, for I am your God. I will strengthen you, yes, I will help you. I will uphold you with My righteous right hand.

–Isaiah 41:10 (NKJV)

"How ya doin', boy?" Our all-purpose farm dog, Freckles, had come to meet me as I stepped outside one March evening, just before dark. "You're such a faithful boy, always here to help me with the chores." I dug my gloved fingers into his yellow, medium-length hair, still thick with his winter coat.

My companion charged forward, whining, then returned to me and catapulted into the air, directly in front of me. More whining.

"What's up, Freckles?"

Normally, during our walks to the barn, Freckles positions his head beneath my left hand for as much petting and scratching as possible. This evening, though, he continued his urgent, back and forth pattern, prompting me to hurry. It was not the first time Freckles had alerted me to trouble. Several years prior, on a dark evening, he had scratched on our back screen door, a huge no-no, until I went outside to find that my horses had escaped and got into my garden. Another time he whined and ran back and forth like this, he was alerting me to a pack of coyotes in our pasture.

"What's wrong, boy, I don't see anything amiss." All gates in the barn and pastures were shut, and the sheep were resting, chewing their cuds. "You must be mistaken, Freckles."

Then out of the corner of my eye I saw a flash of brown fur. Freckles saw it, too, and darted after the bold coyote visiting the fenced area where my hay is stored. Freckles chased the intruder out into the field. The coyote was still running for its life when Freckles returned, wagging his tail and looking a little coy as if he wanted to say, "Can't you just trust me?"

"You are such a good boy, Freckles. You spotted danger, even before the sheep did." I gave him an extended scratching and praise fest. "You're the best mutt a family could have."

Freckles's usefulness never ceases to amaze me. He is an odd mix of breeds: Yellow Lab, Sharpei, Heeler, and Border Collie. At least that is what the folks on the corner giving away puppies while the Fourth of July parade was getting ready to begin, told us. And I believe it. Who would make up such a claim?

At night, Freckles, so named for the brown dots on his nose, barks to keep coyotes at bay. He barks and runs out toward the intruders to send them packing, but he is also smart enough not to run too far out into the field when it is full of coyotes. He knows that he could be attacked and hurt or killed, should he allow himself to be lured too far from the barnyard.

Freckles is also a decent herder. He has learned to run out into the pasture when I say "Go get the sheep." Initially, he ran out and cut through the sheep, frightening and splitting the flock. By going out into the field with him, I was able to teach him to circle around the far side of the flock and push the sheep together toward home. Unlike finely-trained herding dogs that can place sheep where commanded with precision, Freckles' herding skills are limited to bringing in the flock at night. I believe that his shortcomings as a herder have more to do with my inability to teach him than his willingness to learn. Freckles is also very, very good at spotting trouble or finding missing animals. I've had stranded lambs out in the pasture, and he is able to find them, using his whine to signal me.

From the time I step out of the house until I go back inside, Freckles is either by my side or doing what I ask him to do. His constant presence is a comfort and help to me. Freckles may be "just a dog," but his faithfulness and behaviors remind me of God's promises in Isaiah 41:10.

Even more comforting than the helpful companionship of a sheep dog is the Lord's promise—and the reality—that he is always with us. My faithful Shepherd's admonition not to fear, together with the constant presence and help of his Holy Spirit, give me confidence. At times when I begin to fear, I am actually doubting God and believing Satan. For that reason, I will purpose not to be afraid.

Freckles takes responsibility for our sheep and our farmstead. He watches tirelessly for unwelcome intrusions and barks ferociously to chase away what does not belong. While I sleep, my dog fights battles I know nothing about, creating a safe zone around our house and barnyard. How much more the Good Shepherd and his angels engage in spiritual warfare on my behalf. When I give the Good Shepherd his rightful place in my life, he takes responsibility for my spiritual welfare and well-being. *I will not be dismayed, for he is my God.*

Nothing that happens to me is a surprise to God. I am reassured that my Shepherd has my back. No matter what happens to me or those I love, he will even weave our brokenness into the fabric of perfect life in him.

Finally, even in my struggles and calamities, my Shepherd assures me of victory as I walk in his ways and in his presence. When the Lord declares, "I will uphold you with my righteous right hand," he is referring to the victory he won for us on the cross. While at times God's justice may seem delayed, and I may be tempted in certain situations to give in to fear and dismay, in due time, his grace will prevail!

He guards and guides, rescues and reassures.

–Marilyn

To Ponder:

- What can I do when I don't *feel* that God is with me?
- In what ways do I need victory in my life today? While I wait for resolution of my present circumstance, my faith may be strengthened by recalling the times my Good Shepherd has given me unexpected victories in the past.
- About what things in particular do I want God to "have my back?" Will I release those things to him and trust his promises to always be with me and strengthen me?

To Pray:

Thank you, victorious Shepherd, that you are always with me and that I never need to be dismayed. Thank you for taking responsibility for my well-being, for providing, protecting, and coming alongside me by your Holy Spirit. Thank you that your plan for my life is thoroughly good, as you are. Thank you for your promises of mercy and justice, and for your real and present help as I trust in you.

23
LEADER BEWARE

My people have been lost sheep; their shepherds have led them astray and caused them to roam on the mountains. They wandered over mountain and hill and forgot their own resting place. All who found them have devoured them.

–Jeremiah 50:6-7a (NIV)

This is so unfair, I thought as I stormed into our green, two-story farmhouse from the road where the lumbering yellow school bus had stopped a few minutes earlier to drop off my sisters and me. My friends get to go home after school and ride their shiny bicycles down smooth, paved roads or watch cartoons or read books. I have to go look for sheep. Why can't my parents just leave them in the pen?

In my room I changed from school clothes to chore clothes, which consisted this time of a shirt, heavy sweat-shirt, and jeans—all secondhand and well worn. I ran down the stairs and to the back porch, where I added a coat and gloves. The November afternoon had gone from crisp to cold. The sun was sinking toward the horizon, giving us precious little time to scour the fields, where the sheep had grazed all day, for stragglers. My younger sister Shelly joined me. We caught, bridled, and jumped on our horses, glad for the warmth of their backs on our legs.

"I'll ride the beet field. You do the corn field," I called to Shelly as we left the horse pen, heading in opposite directions.

"OK." Shelly was too cold to notice my bossiness.

We enjoyed riding horses, but this was not a pleasure ride. We split up to cover more than two-hundred acres twice as fast. The movement of my mare's lope beneath me seemed to ease away my sense of injustice over my having to work while my "town" friends enjoyed what I presumed were easy lives. I knew that to make our Northern Colorado sheep and crop farm profitable, my parents had to be resourceful. In spring and summer our flock of sheep ate green pasture, in fall and early winter they ate crop stubble; and when all field forage was gone, we fed the sheep baled hay. Grazing crop stubble, which is the stalk and any grain or other residual left after a crop has been harvested, made use of something that would otherwise go to waste. Grazing stubble also preserved our precious resources of hay, so that the valuable baled hay could be sold or used later in the season. As I scanned the furrowed ground, I also remembered my mother telling me that the grazing sheep's small, cloven hooves broke down the stubble they didn't eat and left their manure. Both were very important for enriching the soil for the next year's crop.

Forty minutes later, hands stiff from cold and face numb from the wind, I was back at the horse pen. "Find anything?" I yelled at my sister, who was turning out her horse.

"Nope. You?"

"Nothing."

Riding the fields in the cold and impending dark was not a chore either of us relished, yet we did it because it had to be done (and because our parents made us). Although I grumbled about checking the fields in the cold, I was diligent. As I moved past bumps and lumps in the ground, often I would stop, turn around and go back, just to be certain it was a clump of dirt or stalks, not an emaciated lamb lying between the rows. I knew that if I was not careful in my job, a stranded lamb would end up dinner for a pack of coyotes.

As an adult I came to realize that checking the fields for marooned sheep had taught me valuable lessons about effective leadership. Here are three leadership principles I gleaned from checking the fields horseback as a young teen.

First, I learned that I alone was responsible for finding any sheep still in the field. Since Shelly and I divided the land to be searched so that we could finish sooner, the buck stopped with each of us for any lingering sheep. When I became the leader of people, whether in the work place, within our 4-H club, of my own children or in another setting, I knew the importance of not leaving any to fend for themselves. I know that just like leaving a lone sheep in the stubble field can be deadly, the consequences of not seeing to the safety of those to whom God has entrusted me can be dire. I regularly check on my "sheep." How are they, really? Do they need my help?

Next, I learned the importance of equipping people I mentor to be ready for the task assigned them. Just as one sheep left alone in a huge, unfenced stubble field is highly vulnerable to attack from predators, people untrained for an assignment are vulnerable to discouragement and eventual failure. Those who look to me as their leader are not "safe" until they have the tools and skills they need to be successful and, in turn, to lead others.

Finally, I learned that leadership may require me to do unpleasant tasks that are rarely glamorous. In the same way I served those sheep by looking out for their safety, effective leaders first must serve their followers, putting their own comfort and convenience second. I may prefer to listen to an audio book while driving in the car or working in my garden, but because I want to keep communication open with my daughter, I resist the temptation to do what I want, so that I can be a servant by listening to her.

In the above passage from Jeremiah, not only have the shepherds not looked after their sheep, they have intentionally led them to places where they will be devoured. Any experienced shepherd reading this Scripture will think, *Yikes, that is a vulnerable place for sheep, wandering night and day without a sheep fold, a shepherd, or a protection dog. It is only a matter of time before these sheep are devoured by predators.*

God will hold such leaders responsible. Matthew 18:6 severely warns those who would lead the vulnerable astray, saying "it would be better for them to have a large millstone hung around their necks and to be drowned in the depths of the sea." Leaders are held to a higher standard.

Seize the opportunity and lead well.

–Marilyn

To Ponder:

- In what ways and to whom am I a leader?
- How can I better serve and teach those I lead?
- Are those I consider my leaders doing an effective job? If not, how can I help them be better leaders? Or is it time to find a new leader?

To Pray:

Good and perfect Shepherd, help me to be the leader I need to be for those who look to me for guidance. Let me be more like you. Help me learn that the secret of being a good leader is being a servant to those I lead. Also, help me learn from the leaders you have put in my life.

Care of innocent lambs reminds us of how important it is to do the right thing.

Newborns can only drink milk; after several weeks they begin to nibble hay or pasture.

24
Milk or Meat?

But solid food belongs to those who are of full age, that is, those who by reason of use have their senses exercised to discern both good and evil.

–Hebrews 5:14 (NKJV)

"Don't stick your fingers in that sheep's mouth; you might get them crunched!" is a common admonition I give to curious folk who, for some unknown reason, want to check inside my sheep's mouths.

When lamb babies are born, they usually have no teeth—just bumpy gums revealing the tooth nubbins under the bottom gum line. Why not the top gum line, also, you ask? Because they have no upper teeth in the front; but in the back they have grinders, and you do not want to get your fingers caught back there. Boy! Does that ever hurt!

At birth, the complete digestive system of a lamb is not yet functioning. These parts are not fully operational until the lambs are fifty to sixty days old. Because of this, the babies drink their mothers' milk to supply their nutritional needs. Soon after birth, they may be able to eat a very digestible supplemental feed, such as "creep feed." As lambs begin to nibble on dry feeds, the rumen and reticulum become naturally inoculated with microorganisms which stimulate the growth and development of these first two stomachs. This action is vital for a lamb's growth. A ewe's milk is very rich and high in protein, giving her lambs a healthy start. When observing a flock of lambs, it is easy to see which lambs lack sufficient milk.

This whole scenario reminds me of when we first become believers, children of our heavenly Shepherd. Our "digestive system" is not yet developed and we need simple nourishment that we can understand and apply to our lives as new, or baby, Christians. Yet we need rich and strengthening food which will help us grow and progress in our understanding of the Word. We need good and reliable teachers who will coach and train us in our walk with the Lord so our growth will not be impeded by weak, or false, teaching.

In a flock of sheep, if a ewe is lacking milk due to sickness, death, or possibly genetics, artificial milk must be provided for her babies. The best choice is a surrogate mother, whether another ewe or a goat. If no surrogate mother is available, I purchase dry, ewe-milk replacer, mix the powder with warm water, and feed the orphan baby with a bottle. Shepherds attach special nipples to the bottle. These nipples, made to imitate those of the ewes', help the lamb adapt to the bottle. It is so important not to over feed a bottle lamb, as they have a tendency to get a disease commonly known as over-eating disease or enterotoxemia, which can be fatal.

When a lamb nurses, it constantly butts the ewe's udder, stimulating her to "let down" her milk. What a hilarious sight it is to watch half-grown twin lambs nursing and butting vigorously as their poor mother's entire hind end is lifted off the ground. Their tails wiggle with delight at finding delicious nutrition. Without milk, lambs cannot survive. Similarly, without the initial "baby food" for new believers, it is difficult for them to survive, grow, and mature. Enthusiastic new believers constantly search for truth and ways in which they can flourish as Christians. Some are so passionate in their newfound life, it is a joy to watch their eagerness.

I have observed some lambs who were not receiving

enough milk from their mothers, or perhaps they had been rejected by their moms. They have figured out how to sneak in behind other ewes of the flock when the moms are preoccupied with eating. The lambs dive in from the rear and grab a few mouthfuls of stolen milk. Some ewes will tolerate this thievery; these babies know which ewes to target for lunch. As the lambs mature, they seek solid food in addition to milk. Until the lambs are weaned by the shepherd or by their mothers, they will continue to drink milk. Then they eat only forages and sometimes grain.

Like the lambs, baby Christians need milk to grow. We need to learn to understand the basics of the Bible. It is important to feed on material we understand before we get involved in the complicated issues that confuse us. As we mature, our minds become ready for more intricate truths and knowledge, the "meat of the Word."

We need to be careful who and what fills our minds concerning spiritual matters. There is a lot of good material written and taught by devoted Christian leaders; but we are wise not to absorb anything not backed up by God's Word, the Bible. We grow and mature as we feed on the meat of the Word, after we have developed a foundation on the milk of the Word. This prepares us for any coming storm. Just like my lambs, feed on the basics first, then advance to maturity.

–Millie

To Ponder:

- Am I in the "milk stage" of my Christian life, or am I ready to start digesting the "meat," the more complicated foodstuffs of the Scriptures?
- Do I desire to grow, or am I satisfied to stay where I am in my walk with the Lord?
- Do I have a person to shepherd me and help me grow in all stages of my spiritual life?
- Am I mature enough to discern good from evil? If not, who can shepherd or disciple me in developing this discernment?

To Pray:

Heavenly Father, thank you for providing shepherds here on earth who are willing to help me grow in my spiritual life. Help me never become so contented or complacent that I quit maturing. Prepare my mind to absorb the meat of your Word as I move on from the milk stage. Show me your will for my life; help me renew my commitment to you each day, and turn me aside when I start down a wrong path. I want to be as excited about learning from your Word as the lambs are about feasting from their mothers' udders.

25
WATCH, FOR NIGHT IS COMING

Watch therefore, for you do not know what hour your Lord is coming. –Matthew 24:42 (NKJV)

I must work the works of Him who sent Me while it is day: the night is coming when no one can work. –John 9:4 (NKJV)

As the sun sank lower behind the majestic Rocky Mountains that towered west of her ranch, her anxious eyes scanned the eastern fields for her "girls." Worried thoughts entered her mind: Were they lost? Did coyotes grab them? Could they be injured or even dead? *They never come home this late.*

Just before panic set in, seven contented ewes appeared on the horizon. As relief flooded her mind, a huge sigh escaped her lips. "Whew! You girls finally got here. Why are you so late!"

My friend Edith lived on a huge ranch (thousands of acres) on the prairie, miles north of our farm. Her husband grew wheat and owned a sizable herd of beautiful cattle. Edith was one of the most industrious women I have known. Her home was recognized far and wide for hospitality to friends and strangers alike.

But her passion was her sheep. Though her herd was small, numbering only seven head, they were the epitome of loved and spoiled animals. At dawn's first light, Edith journeyed out to the sheep corral, opened the door and wished her "ladies" a good day. Hastily, the ewes headed out for a full day of grazing and resting on the vast prairie and wheat land.

Each evening she greeted them back home with a friendly welcome and cool drink of water. In the safety of the corral they rested all night, eager to begin the routine again when the sun arose.

It was amazing that Edith's sheep never became lunch for the coyotes that roamed the fields—probably because coyotes tend to do their hunting at night and, at that time, there was an abundance of prairie dogs, jack rabbits, gophers and other delectable "goodies" that were easier for coyotes to kill and eat. Edith's concern for her "ladies" is understandable when they did not come home until night was nearing. She did not let the ewes out during the periods when they had small lambs, as the little ones were sure to be devoured by the wily coyotes.

At one time, I had a car bumper sticker that read, "Eat American lamb; 10,000 coyotes can't be wrong!"

When it was time for Edith's lambs to be born, her ewes were confined in a smaller pen near the house and then locked up at night in the cozy shed. Not only the ewes stayed in the shed at night, but Edith could also be found bedded down on a bale of straw with her pillow and blanket, waiting for the lambs to arrive. Even as she dozed, her sensitive ears caught the sounds of any ewe experiencing labor pains. Ewes develop what we call a "lambing baa" shortly before giving birth. When we hear that call, we know birth is imminent.

I think our Shepherd waits and listens for his lambs to arrive in his fold, as well. He is anxious for us to "come home" before the dark night arrives and it is too late. His lambs are always in danger of being snatched by the enemy, especially when we linger in the "dark" without him by our side. How Edith loved her sheep! She worked so hard taking care of them, and she also realized that our Lord compared us to sheep. In closely working with and living with our sheep, both she and I understood why the Lord calls us sheep and he our Shepherd.

It is so important that we watch for Jesus' return and that we are ready for his coming. Time is drawing short when it will be too late. His desire is for us to share him with the world and encourage others to watch for him and be ready for his appearance. Our Shepherd is watching and waiting for us to "come home." The world is full of people who have never heard of Jesus, others who have heard but rejected him, and others who do not understand the implications of not knowing him as their Shepherd. It is up to us to help fulfill this mission. Many souls will go into eternity without Jesus because we didn't share our testimony with them.

Our heavenly Shepherd provides all we need. He is watching for souls to turn their hearts toward him. II Peter 3:9 tells us, "He is not willing that any should perish." The "night" is coming rapidly when our chances to share Christ will be lost. He is watching and waiting for his lambs to come home. Don't let the "coyotes" waylay you, his sheep, as you gather up other lambs and travel home to the safety of the Shepherd's corral.

–Millie

To Ponder:

- Picture the masses of human beings who will *not* find their way "home" to the fold, even though our Heavenly Shepherd is anxiously awaiting them. What can/should I do to help them find the way?
- To what is the "night" in these verses referring?
- How can we compare the "lambing baa" to the imminent birth of one of the Shepherd's lambs?
- How long will our heavenly Shepherd wait for his lambs to come home to the sheepfold?

To Pray:

Dear Keeper of the Gate, thank you for providing the path so I can find my way home to the "fold." Thank you for giving your life in my place. Please give me a burden for those who are lost and wandering around aimlessly, seeking to fill their empty hearts. Keep me mindful there are lost souls all around me, not just in countries far away. Fill my mouth with the words you want me to say to those folks whose hearts are open to hear about you. Thank you for waiting and watching patiently for your lambs to come home.

Lambs are typically 5 to 8 pounds at birth.

Author and shepherd Marilyn Wentz shows a lamb to a 4-H'er interested in becoming a veterinarian.

26
Hear the Shepherd's Voice

The voice of the Lord is powerful; the voice of the Lord is full of majesty.

–Psalm 29:4 (NKJV)

"Welcome to the world, baby." These are often the first words my newborn lambs hear as they arrive during the birth process.

From the time my lambs are born, I talk to them so they will recognize my voice. This is conducive to making them gentler and not afraid when they hear me speak. It is a valuable tool to use when working with sheep. When they are out in the pasture, I can call them into the corral when it is time to close the gate at night. They come running to me when I beckon them at feeding time, anxious to find their supper. Sometimes one or more will escape from the pen and wander in another field or even on the road. What a blessing it is to be able to walk up to them or call them back home—especially since sheep don't do well with "chase and catch."

One time I took a friend with me into the lambing barn to see the new lambs. He entered ahead of me. Immediately all the ewes in the jugs ran to the rear of their pens, attempting to escape from this stranger with the unfamiliar voice. Then I spoke to the ewes. They calmed down and came to me spontaneously.

The young fellow was amazed. "The sheep really do know the shepherd's voice!"

An exception to this rule may be when bottle lambs are involved. At times when a ewe is unable to feed her baby it will need to be fed with replacement milk in a bottle. The mother may have rejected the baby, does not have enough milk, is sick or dead, and a surrogate mother is not available. Whatever the situation, the baby has to eat. A bottle lamb will approach anyone if there is a possibility of being fed.

Several years ago, I had a bottle lamb that faithfully came for his meal every time. One morning he didn't show up—unheard of for a bottle lamb unless it is sick, injured, or has died. Though I searched hours for him, he was nowhere to be found. The next morning there he was, happily wagging his tail, anticipating his breakfast.

The oil-field workers across the road had been spending their down time admiring my sheep. I assume the bottle lamb had approached one of the workers, who "borrowed" him for the evening, perhaps to entertain his family at home. I was glad the lamb was returned to the fold, unhurt and happy.

Most of my sheep have numbered ear tags. I always call my favorites by name, and it is obvious they learn their names, because when I call out a name, the proper ewe will lift her head and look at me. They do listen to the shepherd. When I was twelve years old, my dad bought me my first lamb. I named her Teddy Bear and we became solid friends. For hours on end we played together, and she learned several tricks. She could shake hands, kneel down, lie down, and stand up with her front feet on my chest. We even played hide-and-seek. I would tell her, "Lie down." Then I would go elsewhere in our yard to hide. When I called her, Teddy Bear scrambled to her feet and searched until she found me. She was a good listener and playmate. Who says sheep are stupid!

As I write this, a group of my daughter's lambs are

grazing on our pasture. When they first arrived, I kept them in a small part of the corral and talked to them a lot, in order to get them used to listening to my voice. My voice calmed them and removed much of their fear. Though they are somewhat aloof around me, they do come running in from the pasture at night when I call—if they are near enough to hear my voice.

Our heavenly Shepherd speaks to us, too. But we are not always listening. He speaks to us through the Bible, through our pastor-shepherds and through godly friends. He also guides us through our consciences and through the voice of the Holy Spirit. Many years ago, I was teaching a Sunday School lesson to children aged five and six. Our lesson was on prayer. We learned that when we pray, God always answers "yes" or "no" or "wait a while." I asked the children if any of them had heard God answer a prayer.

Little Kelly wanted to tell of her experience. "Last week I was riding my pony, Blackie, and he pooped on the driveway. I prayed, 'God what should I do?' I heard God say to me, 'Get a shovel and clean it up.'"

She was so sincere, I had no doubt she had heard God's voice.

Our Shepherd does not always speak in a loud voice. In I Kings 19:11-12, the prophet Elijah did not hear God's voice in a powerful wind, or in an earthquake, or in a terrific fire; but he did hear it as a "still, small voice." We often lose patience waiting to hear that voice and also expect it to be definitive in its message. Learn to "wait" and listen for the Shepherd's voice. He will answer you.

–Millie

To Ponder:

- Consider various ways in which God speaks to his lambs.
- When I hear God's voice, am I willing to be obedient to his plans?
- Why does the Good Shepherd want to speak to me?
- Sometimes the Lord just wants us to shut up, be quiet, and wait!

To Pray:

Loving Father, I know you have wanted to be my Shepherd since long before I was born. Please help me to be an obedient child of yours and learn to know and follow your will and guidance for my life. Help me to listen for what you want me to hear and to be patient and wait for your powerful and majestic voice. Forgive me when I think I know better than you. I praise you for being a God who speaks!

27
Wholly Accepted by the Great Shepherd

But if we walk in the light, as he is in the light, we have fellowship with one another, and the blood of Jesus, his Son, purifies us from every sin.

–I John 1:7 (NIV)

The lumbering yellow school bus dropped off my sisters and me in front of our two-story farmhouse. Anxious to see if any new lambs had been born that crisp February day, I changed from my school clothes into well-worn chore clothes and headed to the barn. The lambing barn was a white clapboard shed that my parents had moved to our property from a neighboring farm. It had windows on the south side to let in a bit of light, and when I flung open the door, I breathed in the earthy odors of straw and alfalfa hay. Newborns bleated their "Notice me, Mama" cries to their attentive mothers. I shut the door to the creaky lambing-barn door, having been told the importance of keeping the chill out of the unheated building.

Inside, I stopped short. My mother sat on her haunches, holding the back legs of a dead baby lamb with her left hand, pulling its hide toward its head with her right hand.

"Help me skin this lamb." Mother beckoned, seeing my hesitation. "It died two days ago, and I have been trying to get its mother to accept the lamb rejected by #32 over there." She gestured to a jug, one of the individual enclosures we use for a ewe and its newborns, farther back in the lambing barn.

I nodded, aware that #32 had given birth to triplets but was unable to feed all three of her lambs.

"Here, hold the back legs."

I grasped the bloodied back hooves.

She gave the hide a long, firm jerk, pulling it to the lamb's neck, then used a knife to cut the hide off at the neck. "This is the last thing I know to try." As she said those words, her voice broke.

My mother had attempted to graft the triplet onto the ewe who had lost her lamb by forcing the ewe to stand still while the new lamb nursed. She did this four to six times a day, hoping the ewe's individual scent would pass from the milk to the body of the new lamb. Sometimes this process fools the ewe into accepting a lamb that is not hers. This time it did not.

Even as a sixth-grader, I knew that when a newborn lamb wet from the birth process is presented to a ewe that did not give birth to it, the ewe will typically accept the lamb as her own. Once the orphan's coat is dry, it is more difficult to get the new mother to accept it. As an adult, I still don't know what chemically or biologically happens throughout this process, but I have observed that as a ewe licks off its newborn lamb immediately upon giving birth to it, the scent seems to write itself on the ewe's memory. This scent helps each ewe identify her lamb when it is young and even into adulthood. When ewes and their weaned offspring are reunited, sometimes months later, they are able to identify each other by smell.

Some ewes will accept any lamb—wet or dry—as their own. Most, however, will reject an orphan lamb that is more than several hours old. Rather than simply ignore the orphan, the ewe will butt the "intruder" to prevent it from nursing. This is nature's way of ensuring that a mother feeds only her own lambs. Otherwise, the more aggressive lambs would get more than their share of milk from multiple mothers, and the weaker lambs would starve to death.

Even now, as I recall that poignant scene of a bloodied hide ripped away from a carcass of defined muscles, sinew, and tendons, I am in awe of the parallel between what it took for the ewe to accept the orphaned lamb and what our Shepherd did to make me acceptable to the Father.

On that February day my mother had skinned the ewe's own lamb and placed its hide over the orphan's body. In this way, the orphan looked and smelled like the ewe's dead lamb. The ewe's first reaction to the lamb with the new hide was one of confusion, but she soon accepted the lamb as hers and eventually, the skin of the dead lamb was removed. It was not the only time my mother used this last-ditch effort to graft an orphan to an adoptive mother.

Anytime I question how a holy, perfect God accepts me with all my flaws, the picture of the skinned orphan lamb comes to mind. When God the Father looks at me, he doesn't see the Marilyn who has again had to ask forgiveness for losing patience with her daughter. He chooses to see the hide of Jesus, his perfect son, covering me.

Unlike the ewe, he is not confused or deceived about the switch from sinner to perfect Lamb of God. He planned from the beginning of time to make this exchange. My perfect, holy and just God can fully accept me as his child, because Jesus took the punishment I deserve. He redeemed me with his own blood shed on the cross.

Just like the ewe that refused to accept the orphaned lamb in its own hide, any attempt I might make to be good enough to deserve salvation on my own merit is insufficient. In fact, according to Isaiah 64:6, all of my attempts to be good enough to deserve salvation are like "filthy rags." Once I acknowledge my utter dependence on Jesus for salvation, I am forgiven for all my sin.

This redemptive sacrifice is available to anyone, but the believer must get under the hide of Jesus, the sacrificed Lamb of God. While God will allow anyone to put on Jesus' redemptive hide, he will not force anyone to wear it. I must choose to get under the skin, to wear it, and to let the smell and feel of it overtake me.

–Marilyn

To Ponder:

- Am I trusting the blood of Jesus and that alone for my salvation, or am I trying to be good enough to come before God without putting on his Son's skin?
- How can I quit struggling with trying to be good enough for God's salvation and rest in his provision?

To Pray:

Good Shepherd, thank you for sending your Son, Jesus, to die for me and to provide the blood covering for all my sin. I accept (or have accepted) this incredible gift. Help me live as a forgiven person, and help me have an attitude of forgiveness toward others. May I always remember that you love and fully accept me when I come to you with a repentant heart.

28
Contentment

Not that I speak in regard to need, for I have learned in whatever state I am, to be content.

–Philippians 4:11 (NKJV)

Let your conduct be without covetousness; be content with such things as you have. For He Himself has said, "I will never leave you nor forsake you.

–Hebrews 13:5 (NKJV)

"Peeeuuuuuuww; what is that awful smell?" Katie was standing in front of the "fair lamb" when her project emitted a loud burp, releasing all the gases that had accumulated in his stomach, or stomachs I should say.

"Katie, do you know what happens when sheep eat? Do you know what they eat, and how a sheep utilizes its food to turn it into meat and energy?" I asked. "The putrid smell you just got a whiff of was the gas produced as your lamb digested the food he just ate."

God created sheep in a unique way, just as each of us is designed in an incomparable fashion. A sheep has four stomachs or, more accurately, four compartments in its stomach. Each stomach cavity serves a special purpose. Sheep are known as "grazers," a subcategory of ruminants, which means they are meant to eat forages such as grass, weeds, hay, etc., although they are able to consume grain and other foodstuffs, too. Except for the "grinding teeth" at the back of their mouths, they have teeth only on the lower part of their gums. With these front teeth, and the help of their tongues, they are able to cut and pull in their food.

After swallowing a mouthful, the food enters the first stomach, the rumen, where minute microorganisms begin to attack and break it down, resulting in fermentation. As it moves on to the second stomach, the reticulum, the food is further broken down and fermented. After the sheep has temporarily satisfied its hunger, it will find a comfortable resting spot and lie down (or stand contentedly). When a flock of sheep are lying down and appear to be resting, they are often chewing, even when they apparently are not in the process of eating. They really are re-eating the food they just took in; by now it is called chewing their cud.

At this point the sheep burps and regurgitates a chunk of the broken-down food and begins chewing it again. When the cud is sufficiently pulverized, the sheep swallows it again, and it continues on through the other stomachs, called the omasum and the abomasum, to finish the digestive process. A large quantity of gas called methane is produced in the rumen and during the cud-chewing phase, the sheep burps frequently. This is the putrid smell Katie noticed as she stood in front of her lamb.

If, for some reason, sheep are unable to release this gas, it can build up in the four stomachs, causing extreme pain and even death. Sheep may spend several hours a day chewing their cuds. During this time they appear to be very content.

Ideally, the shepherd provides plenty of fresh, clean water. Of course, in some situations the sheep are near a water supply only at the end of the day; but regardless of timing, they must have water. How content they appear, after spending a day grazing and chewing their cuds, to now have a good long drink of refreshing water!

When the ewes are lying down, lambs often rest and sleep on their mothers' backs. Not only does this warm their little bodies when it is cold, but it gives them a sense of security. Since their first two stomachs are not functional at a very young age, their bodies are not able to process the same feed their mothers do. Therefore, they must receive life-sustaining milk until their stomachs can utilize solid foods.

God has given sheep an amazing sense of prediction. Before a storm, sheep seem to stuff themselves with food, whether it be pasture grass or hay fed in the corral. They seem to be preparing for an extended time when food will not be available. However, they will also stuff themselves with grain if given the opportunity, and this is not good. (I can't condemn them too much as I sometimes stuff myself with ice cream/chocolate, and that is not good, either.) When sheep consume too much grain at one time, lactic acid is produced in the rumen; and the drop in pH can make sheep very sick. Overeating grain, green alfalfa, or other feed can cause death.

Most shepherds make sure their sheep's heavy wool coats are shorn off once or twice a year. This makes them more comfortable in hot weather. It also facilitates the process of the newborn lambs finding their first meal. If the wool is too long, a baby may suck on a clump of wool instead of the nipple which is hidden by a dense coat of fleece.

There are instances when we read something in the Bible that seems too complicated to absorb. It takes time, concentration, and help from a biblical scholar before we can understand what God may be saying to us. Like the sheep's digestive system, we are overwhelmed until suddenly we "get it." Then we chew it over and over until it becomes part of us and helps us grow and mature.

The Lord has supplied all we need for our contentment. Of course, some have more than others, some abundantly more. We are so blessed to live in this country where we make our own decisions on where we live, what we eat, activities we enjoy, where we fellowship, etc. We can rest warmly and securely on the promises of the Lord. He will provide.

The apostle Paul spent a good part of his Christian life in prison, or at least as a prisoner, yet he claimed to be content in whatever state he found himself. Furthermore, the writer to the Hebrews admonishes us not to covet what others have, but to be content with what we have. He reminds us that God the Father said, "I will never leave you nor forsake you." What more convincing do we need in order to choose contentment?

–Millie

To Ponder:

- Am I content with the "things" the Lord has bestowed on me?
- Do I really believe the Lord has given me everything I need?
- Hasn't the Lord given me a lot of stuff I really don't need (but maybe I want)?
- Do I confuse my "wants" and "needs"?
- Is it difficult to not want more than I have or something different from what I have?
- What do I need in order to be content?

TO PRAY:

My Shepherd Provider, thank-you for giving me all that I need. In your omniscience you know me and will take care of me. Help me to find satisfaction in the things you have given me, and please help me be content and not covet things that others have. Like a lamb on its mother, I find comfort, warmth, and security as I rest on you.

Shearing time

29
Undivided Loyalty

No one can serve two masters; for either he will hate the one and love the other, or else he will be loyal to the one and despise the other. You cannot serve God and mammon.

–Matthew 6:24 (NKJV)

"Lucy, what have you done!"

This Suffolk ewe had looked large during her pregnancy, but not *that* big. Here she was, lovingly cleaning *four* newborn babies! Assuming she would not be able to care for the whole "litter," I waited until they dried off and had their first sip of the thick yellow colostrum that is so vital for a healthy start. Hesitantly I chosc a lamb (they all appeared strong and healthy), discreetly removed him from the lambing pen and placed him in a pen as far away as I could. He would have to be my bottle baby now, since there was not another ewe on which he could be grafted. Generally, we can only graft a lamb onto a ewe who has recently given birth to a single lamb or who has recently lost her own lamb. At that time I didn't have a ewe who fit either category.

Sometimes we had a ewe raise three lambs at once, but this was the first set of quadruplets born in my flock. With just two nipples, sheep do very well to feed three lambs. When triplets are born, I keep a close eye on them. Usually the ewe will stand happily feeding two at a time. Then, without warning, she will take a few steps forward to give the third lamb a chance to eat. (Do you think sheep can count, and reason?) That third baby is ready and waiting and wastes no time in diving in to get its share of the milk. A ewe does this several times, until all three of their tummies are satisfied or until Mama knows they've had enough. Ewes feeding three babies receive extra grain in order to boost their milk supply. Could four lambs get an adequate amount of milk? I didn't think so.

However, the separated lamb would have nothing to do with drinking milk from a bottle. He hollered incessantly for his own mother, and she in turn, bellowed for him. The clamor of baas became extremely annoying. In frustration I moved him farther away, outside with the other sheep; but Lucy knew he was missing from her pen and persistently called for him. He finally drank a little milk from the bottle, just enough to keep from starving to death; but he wanted his mom and nothing else would do. It seemed like his mother could count, because she wouldn't give up trying to redeem her "lost" baby.

"Bring back my other baby; he is mine and you know it," Lucy seemed to say. "I won't stop yelling until I have him here, where he belongs."

Lucy continued to care for her other three, and they were happy not to share with the fourth brother; but the ewe was inconsolable. Finally, after several days, I admitted defeat. "OK, Lucy, you win. You can have your fourth lamb back, but you need to let me supplement him with a bottle."

I put the lamb back in the pen with his delighted mother and three siblings. Still believing the ewe surely could not feed four lambs, I tried supplementing all of the lambs with a bottle, but no one was interested. They grew and thrived in their happy little family and it looked like Lucy wore a smug grin on her face that seemed to say, "See, I told you so."

What a miracle. Lucy and her lambs even got their picture along with a write-up in a local farm magazine, since quads are not an everyday occurrence.

Unlike this single-minded ewe, sometimes our loyalty is divided. The Bible clearly states we cannot serve two masters. We desire to be a part of the world and may choose friends who are not a good influence on us. We find it difficult to make decisions when our "self" kicks in. "I should do_____, but I really want to go/do _______." How can we make the right choice? Would we rather have fun doing something that would not be glorifying God, or should we spend our time in obedience to him? How delighted he must be when we make the choice to desire and seek his guidance for our lives. We can have lots of fun in the Christian life as we follow his will. With spiritual nourishment and Christian friends, we can serve only God and become healthy, vibrant lambs of the Good Shepherd's flock.

–Millie

To Ponder:

- Contrast activities that could be considered "serving God" to those that are "serving mammon." Are they the same for everyone?
- To you, what/who is mammon?
- Consider the result of serving God compared to that of serving mammon. Is it possible to serve both? Why or why not? Which gives true joy?

To Pray:

Father in Heaven, my holy Shepherd, open my eyes that I may see what things I am doing that cause you to grieve. Forgive me for the bad decisions I've make. Help me discern good from evil. Lord, please give me an intense desire to learn more about you and follow you more closely. Please fill me with your nourishment that I might grow and be a healthy member of your flock. May the joy of the Lord be my strength!

Spanish conquistadors considered sheep essential, as the sheep provided meat, milk, and wool to the explorers.

30
God Knows Your Pain

Are not two sparrows sold for a copper coin? And not one of them falls to the ground apart from your Father's will. But the very hairs of your head are all numbered. Do not fear therefore; you are of more value than many sparrows.

–Matthew 10: 29-31 (NKJV)

Lambing season, as shepherds call the time when lambs are born, which is typically anytime between January and May, had begun. Three ewes had given birth; twenty four to go.

"Shannon, are you ready to go check the sheep with me before we go to bed?" It was about 9:00 p.m. on a Friday night, so I recruited my preteen daughter to help. I knew I would be up another time or two before the night was over, to check for new lambs or ewes in labor.

"I guess so, Mom." My younger daughter, Shannon, was not yet a teen; but the attitude was in full force.

"Come on, honey, you don't have school tomorrow. You know we have to check for lambs every few hours when it is cold. You don't want lambs to die, do you?"

"I know, Mom." She headed for the garage where we keep our winter chore gear.

Farm-flock shepherds are able to manage lambing time by turning the rams in with the ewes five days short of five months before they want the lambs to start being born. Winter lambing is difficult for the shepherd but has been a tradition for many farm flocks. It enables the lambs to be market ready earlier, when prices are stronger, and winter is a time when farmers have less other work. Ewes will lick their newborn lambs to warm and stimulate them, but a sheep will typically have twins, sometimes triplets, leaving the firstborn lamb/lambs to fend for themselves while she gives birth to the siblings. A newborn lamb can freeze to death in a couple of hours, which requires a dutiful shepherd to check the flock every three to four hours for ewes in labor.

Another lambing situation that requires a shepherd's prompt intervention is an abnormal birth presentation, such as breech lambs, lambs with their heads tucked under their front legs, or lambs that come into the birth canal head first with their front legs back. Sometimes lambs properly positioned are so large that they need an extra pull to be delivered. Making these deliveries is a skill every shepherd must learn, or the veterinary costs will soon exceed the sheep operation's profit.

I had become rather proud of my abilities to deliver lambs with abnormal presentations, but God has a way of mercifully reminding us that all our skills and knowledge mean nothing without his help.

Shannon and I pulled on our hooded sweatshirts, insulated overalls and chunky, chore boots. When we stepped outside into the early February evening, snow was falling. White coated the ground.

"The snow is beautiful. Look at the big flakes."

My daughter shrugged.

"It's a beautiful night, not even any wind," I added.

We stepped into the barn and pulled the door shut behind us. We walked through the barn and into the attached, three-sided shed. An older ewe, ear tag #49, was in labor. I could see tiny hooves protruding from the birth canal, preparing to enter the world.

"Shannon, keep an eye on 49, while I check outside." She

pulled on the old, laboring ewe until she was in a place with clean straw and better light.

While Shannon kept vigil with 49, I checked the jugs to make sure the new babies had eaten. I took my time feeding and giving fresh water to the ewes in the jugs and then went outside to feed the larger flock of pregnant ewes. When I returned to the barn, Shannon was trying to pull 49's lamb. Everything looked in order.

"Go ahead and pull the lamb, so we can make sure they are OK, then get to bed. It's late."

"Mom, something is wrong. I can't get the lamb out."

"Why not?" I could see the baby's nose with the tips of its cloven hooves on either side of the nose. "It is positioned fine. You need to pull harder."

Assuming Shannon's trouble was her inexperience, I gave it a try but was barely able to get my hand into the birth canal. The lamb was presented properly; however, I could not grab anything but its front legs. I first thought the cervix had not fully dilated, a problem I knew how to solve, but nothing I did increased the size of the opening. For the next forty-five minutes, I repeatedly tried to assist in the delivery. I had not encountered such a situation, and I ran out of options.

I called Mom to see if she had any ideas for me. She did not. My hands were bruised and aching from trying to push them through a half-inch, sharp-edged opening. The ewe had gone down onto the ground and not gotten back up. She was alive but very weak.

"Shannon, go inside and call Mr. Schroth." Our neighbor is an experienced shepherd.

Shannon was back in the barn ten minutes later. "He's on his way."

A few minutes later my neighbor entered our barn.

"I'm so sorry to get you out of bed, Bob," I said

"That's OK." Bob is really smart and knows so much

about sheep but his humility is winsome. "Don't know if I can help; whatcha got here?"

Bob examined #49. "Her pelvis has closed. I had a ewe last year with the same thing. First time I'd ever seen it."

"What are my options?" I was pretty sure I knew but wanted to hear it from him.

"If you can get a vet out, you could try an emergency cesarean."

Gulp. I knew the words "emergency" and "cesarean" added up to hundreds of dollars. "She's an old ewe and is already pretty weak from being in labor so long. Even if we had a vet do a cesarean, I doubt we could save the lambs." I assumed she was carrying twins. "I think the humane thing to do is to put her out of her misery."

"I can't disagree. I'd do the same."

"Would you do it for me?

A few minutes later, Bob fired two, well-placed, merciful shots from his .22 caliber pistol into the old ewe's head. She died immediately.

Bob left, and Shannon and I trudged to the house, our bodies exhausted and hearts heavy.

"I'm sorry to have been so impatient with you, Shannon."

"I know, Mom." She was on the verge of tears. "I feel so bad—especially because the lambs died, too."

"Me, too, honey. I hate this part of being a shepherd."

It was 1:00 a.m. before I swung my aching legs into bed. I set the alarm for the next check, four hours later.

It snowed about ten inches that night, making removal of #49's body impossible for nearly a week. Every time I walked past her body, I mourned her death. Had she just been dead when I went out to the pen one day, it would not have bothered me as much. I thought about the two unborn lambs that never lived outside her womb. I thought about all her years of bearing and rearing nice lambs for me. She had not been a special ewe or one of my daughters' show sheep, but still I mourned her passing.

A few days later, Matthew 10:29-31 came to me. After meditating on this scripture, I still felt sadness but not the deep despair I had felt all week over the death of this ewe. I believe the Holy Spirit was telling me that he knew about #49 and her lambs. He also reminded me how very sad he is about the fallen world in which we live. I felt an overwhelming sense of peace and love from our great Shepherd. He reminded me that he is a just God and that he will right all wrongs.

#49 was a ewe, just another sheep some would say, yet I know from scripture that God knew the very moment she and her lambs died. I believe he even grieved over it. How much more does he grieve over sadness and the injustices done to you and me and to all humankind?

–Marilyn

TO PONDER:

- What things in my life or in the lives of others seem unfair?
- Do I ever feel like God doesn't notice or doesn't care about these injustices?
- If I feel like God isn't paying attention, am I wrong? What scriptures tell me that he feels my pain and in due time will right all wrongs?

To Pray:

Great Shepherd, surely you have made humankind with a sense of justice in our hearts. Grant me a sensitivity to your justice in all my dealings with others; yet, Lord, I live in a fallen world that often lacks true and complete justice. Help me to trust in your unconditional, all-knowing love and rest in the assurance that a day is coming when you will right every wrong in the fullness of your kingdom.

Some lambs need a little encouragement to thrive, especially those rejected by their mothers.

31
Love People Even When

Be shepherds of God's flock that is under your care, watching over them—not because you must, but because you are willing, as God wants you to be; not pursuing dishonest gain, but eager to serve; not lording it over those entrusted to you, but being examples to the flock. And when the Chief Shepherd appears, you will receive the crown of glory that will never fade away. –I Peter 5: 2-4 (NIV)

"**Calm down, Lauren**, you're going to hurt your babies." I chided the two-year-old ewe. She had given birth to two nice lambs but would not stand still so they could eat. Instead she circled the pen, knocking them down. "You should understand the routine by now, girl; this is not your first time to have a baby."

I checked to be sure Lauren had milk. She did. I made one last check of Lauren and her babies before leaving the barn that morning. Still jittery, at least she was letting her lambs drink. "That a girl." I tried to encourage her, though I sounded more convinced than I felt.

Several hours later, it was time to check the ewes who had not yet lambed. It was a pleasant February afternoon, but not knowing how long I might be outside, I pulled on my bulky insulated coveralls and donned heavy boots before leaving the house for the barn.

In the barn I immediately noticed something wrong with the male lamb's leg. I hopped into the jug. "What have you done, Lauren? You broke his leg, and it's bad, really bad." The lamb's lower leg was just dangling.

I went to the house and scooped up splinting supplies. Back in the barn, I stretched the lamb across my lap and used popsicle sticks, gauze and a strong, sticky material we call vet wrap, to form a splint. It was not the first time I had done this. I propped the sweet, patient little guy onto his feet then stared at him. He put his weight on three legs and let the fourth, his right back leg, dangle. The popsicle-stick splint was not going to work.

Time to call Dr. Jodie. My veterinarian friend splinted the lamb's leg with a hard plastic piece that ran from the hoof to the hip. She showed me how to re-bandage the leg. I would have to do this often to accommodate the growing lamb.

Returning from the veterinary office, I put the injured lamb by himself in a pen, where I spread fresh straw. "Poor little guy. Your mama has enough milk for you and your sister, but I don't dare put you back into her pen, and I can't leave you out with the rest of the flock, or you'll be trampled." I tried to sound confident and lift his spirits, knowing he'd be very lonely by himself. "Don't worry. I'll bring you a bottle the next time I come."

Initially, I fed the lamb four times a day, decreasing to twice a day at two weeks. Each time I went out to check the flock, he wagged his tail and bleated at me, hobbling to the gate of his pen on his splinted leg. I spent extra time petting and holding him. Caring for this injured lamb consumed as much time as the rest of the work I did to shepherd the other sixty ewes and lambs.

Raising sheep is a passion for me, but it is also a business. I depend on making money for my labors; yet the decision to keep and nurture this lamb was made not from a business point of view, but from the heart. Then, as if good sense and practicality were screaming "I told you so," at about six weeks of age, the lamb contracted a fast-moving virus and died of Enterotoxemia, a bacterial infection.

I felt sad, but also angry. I kicked myself for not putting this lamb down in the beginning. The poor thing experienced so much suffering in his short life, yet I knew if it happened again to another lamb, I would do the same thing all over again.

Working with people can be similarly difficult and heartbreaking. As a 4-H and AWANA leader in my church, I have mentored young people, pouring my life into them, so they can mature and make their own mark on society. Many of these young folks have gone on to be successful, but some have chosen to take selfish paths and to engage in negative patterns of behavior.

When failures occur, I wonder whether I have wasted my time and energy mentoring the individual. What is the use of having poured my heart and soul into so-and-so? However, this is not God's perspective. No one knows the outcome or the pay off, if you will, for the time spent mentoring and helping someone God has brought across our path. If, in his providence, he places such a lamb in my flock, my part is to do all I can to nurture and train "my lambs." The outcome is up to him.

I have learned another lesson from working with both people and sheep. It is very difficult to make sheep go anywhere they are afraid to go. Cattle, horses, even goats can be forced or pushed into an enclosure with enough pressure. Sheep, on the other hand, will turn around and come back toward those pushing them. They are not stubborn, just scared of the unknown. When faced with having to move sheep into an unknown space, a shepherd must go into the space and wait. I have learned to persuade my sheep to follow me by enticing them with a handful of grain. Eventually, one of the less skittish ewes will find the confidence to follow me into the new area. After a lot of waiting and encouraging, the rest of the flock will follow.

People, likewise, don't want to go into places they perceive as frightening or uncertain and dangerous. They need their shepherd to go before them. They will balk at someone standing behind and pressuring them to plunge into something their leader is not willing to do. Can you blame them? An effective leader must be a balance of strength and vulnerability. A good leader is the servant of his or her flock and leads, rather than pushes.

"The crown of glory that never fades away" mentioned in this scripture does not consist of the successes of those we have loved, mentored, and protected. Rather, it is a heavenly reward for my faithfulness to love and guide those whom the Chief Shepherd has entrusted to me, as I leave the results to him.

–Marilyn

TO PONDER:

- In what areas is God calling me to lead others?
- Am I willing to go the extra mile to serve my flock or am I being a lazy leader?
- Am I looking for glory, or loving and leading freely?
- In what ways can I better serve my flock?

TO PRAY:

Thank you, Chief Shepherd, for those you put under my care—family, friends, and others. Renew my courage, discipline, and creativity as a servant-leader. Help me remember the best leader is a servant of all and in God's economy, the first will be last and the last first. Show me others for whom you wish me to be a shepherd, and remind me to look to you, the Great Shepherd, for guidance.

32
You Are Precious to God

Know that the Lord is God. It is he who made us, and we are his; we are his people, the sheep of his pasture.

–Psalm 100:3 (NIV)

I awoke to a deliciously cool morning, a delightful precursor to the very hot July day forecast by the previous evening's news. I jumped out of bed, made a cup of steaming black coffee and carried it to the barn with me. Birds chirped their greetings as I stepped outside my house. Halfway to the barn, my ewe flock heard me coming and moved toward the gate, urging my haste with their baaing and pressing against the gate.

"Yes, yes, ladies and lambs, I know you are anxious to eat your fill of green grass before it gets too hot." I removed the bungee cord from the wire panel gate, lifted it off the ground and swung it out and open to let the sheep rush out. "I am also anxious to get my outdoor work done while it is still cool."

I fed the horses and the dog, checked to make sure the barn cats had food, then cleaned the water receptacles. I stopped and took a deep breath. "OK," I said to myself. "Quit putting it off and just get it done." It was a task I hated but one that had to be done if I was ever going to triumph over the sandbur, cocklebur, and goat head populations. Weeds were one thing, but weeds with harmful stickers in them gave my sheep abscesses and stuck in their wool, making it painful for them and painful for me when I had to handle them. Also, these weeds could choke out the grasses eaten by my livestock.

I piled a five-gallon bucket, a shovel, and a 38-gallon, heavy-duty plastic trash bag in the wheel barrow. I pulled on thick, leather work gloves, grasped the wheel barrow handles and headed for the pasture. Fortunately, the irritating sticker weeds had only spread in limited areas so far. I wheeled to one of those places and told myself I would work just until I had that area cleaned out. I dug out each sticker plant with the shovel, shook off dirt from its roots and dumped it into the five-gallon bucket. When the bucket was overflowing, I used the shovel to tamp down the stickers, and then I dumped the compact pile into the trash bag. It was a workable system.

Sweat trickled down my face and neck. As I toiled in the increasing heat, I took joy in watching my peaceful, grazing flock of sheep. The grass was lush and the sky a bright blue with billowy clouds that promised an afternoon thunderstorm. Yellow, white, pink and purple wildflowers dotted the pasture, where the ewes and lambs moved, heads down grazing from one blade of luscious grass to the next. Occasionally, one of the older ewes would look up and scan the horizon, ensuring no predators lurked.

I continued cutting out the weeds, but the burdensome task was balanced with the delight I felt watching my flock. I knew the serenity of the scene could be broken at any time. Movement as mundane as a startled Cottontail rabbit jumping from behind a bush to hop across the pasture could send the flock running for the protection of the pen.

The joy of the Lord, expressed by the psalmist when he said "We are his people, the sheep of his pasture," made perfect sense to me in that moment. God compares his delight in me and you to a flock of peacefully-grazing sheep.

He could have compared his delight to another animal in his creation. Why not say we are his people, the horses of his stable? Horses (which I am partial to) are beautiful, strong and fast. Surely, the Lord delights in seeing the horses he created. Or, why not compare his delight in us to that of seeing a lion? Male or female, a lion is a powerful and awe-inspiring animal. Or, surely the Lord is delighted to see the soaring eagles he created. They are simultaneously fierce and beautiful. They can soar high and dive powerfully. Their outstretched wings are a wonder to behold.

He could have compared his delight with us to any animal, but in this Psalm, he says I am as pleasing to him as the sheep of his pasture. It is a good reminder that to please him we don't need to be fast and athletic like a horse, powerful like a lion, or beautiful and awe inspiring like an eagle. What pleases him is when we, like the skittish sheep, run to him for everything we need, trusting his sufficiency to supply all our needs.

God does not need my cleverness, my strength, or my outward beauty. He wants my gentle, quiet, yielded spirit. Just as when the sheep runs toward the shepherd for protection, when I surrender to him, he can use me to accomplish his purposes. When he uses me in this way, I am under his complete protection.

Just as you are, know today that you are fully loved by God. He delights in you. As the sheep of his pasture, you are precious to him.

–Marilyn

TO PONDER:

- Do I truly believe I am precious to God just the way I am?
- In what areas of my life do I need to stop working to be something I am not, thinking it will please him?
- What would it look like if I stopped striving to please the Good Shepherd with my own goodness and totally surrendered to him and his good purposes for my life?

TO PRAY:

Good Shepherd, I do not understand how you can love me unconditionally, nor how I in my frail humanity can please you. Help me to follow the gentle, humble sheep's attitude as I seek you and your will for my life. Show me today what I need to surrender to you. Thank you for the privilege, peace, and safety of being a sheep of your pasture.

This Southdown ewe is gentle but alert, concerned that no one harms her precious newborn..

Raising sheep and learning to weave and spin wool were considered patriotic acts during the American Revolution.

33
Dead Sheep

And you he made alive, who were dead in trespasses and sins.

–Ephesians 2:1 (NIV)

"Shelly, why don't you come with me to the neighbor's place to check out the old ensilage pit for anything we might be able to use? People dump all kinds of stuff in there."

Being a scavenger at heart, I'm always on the lookout for other people's castoffs that may be treasures to me. The pit was situated less than two miles from our home, and we had finished our morning chores. It seemed like an adventure my teenage daughter might relish. Besides, the pit was near a sheep feedlot where we could "check out" the lambs.

On that ideal summer day the fluffy, cotton-ball clouds posed no imminent threat of rain. Besides, we wouldn't be gone long; so we set out in our old red-and-white, beat-up pickup truck. Shelly and I rummaged through the pit and claimed a few useful items. (To this day, I have the twelve-by-seventeen-inch baking pan discovered there; now why would someone throw that away!) We realized it was warming up rapidly when sweat began dropping off our foreheads. Perhaps we'd explored enough for one day.

Driving past the sheep feedlot, we noticed several big lambs which, appearing lifeless, had been thrown outside the corral for the rendering truck to haul them away.

"Look!" squealed Shelly. "That one's still breathing."

We bounded from the vehicle and examined the lamb

closely. She certainly gave all appearance of being dead; but as we watched, her sides moved up and down ever so slightly. We checked the other "dead lambs" and three others exhibited the same symptoms. They didn't look alive, but their barely heaving sides proved the contrary. Sad to think these poor creatures would be piled on a truck of dead carcasses for their last ride.

Shelly and I jumped into the truck and hurried home. We called the neighbor to get his permission to take the discarded lambs from his feedlot.

He laughingly quizzed, "What in the world do you want them for? Sure, I don't care."

So we hitched the horse trailer to the pickup and off we roared to retrieve the "dead lambs." Together we dragged four almost lifeless bodies into the horse trailer, but one of them, being "deader" than the others, did pass away before we arrived home.

Once home, we towed the not-quite-dead lambs to the north side of our house, where there was grass and shade. At that time, Marilyn owned a 4-H milk cow that she milked by hand twice a day, and Marla had 4-H hens. In the blender I mixed fresh, rich milk with raw eggs and blended the mixture until smooth. After filling glass coke bottles with the thick, creamy liquid, we held up the lambs' heads, one by one, and poured the liquid into the mouths of severely dehydrated young sheep. We also offered them fresh, cool water which they lustily gulped. Several times a day we infused the recovering lambs with this milk and egg mixture. And we injected them with large doses of Vitamin B.

Then began the therapy. Several times a day I slid my legs under each lamb and lifted it up on my knees, straightening and massaging each inert leg. It was tedious work; but I was determined to save these lambs. It was partly stubbornness on my part, but persistence began to pay off. By the third day, these babies began struggling to get on their feet. Then they worked to toddle around—just like a child learning to take his first steps. I continued the Vitamin B shots and muscle therapy for several days and by the fourth day, we had three new lambs to add to our flock.

I believe all of us are like "dead sheep" in the eyes of God before we come to know him as our Shepherd. The Bible says when we were dead in our trespasses and sins, his Holy Spirit gave us life! It takes his love and persistence to revive us and change us into the sheep of his flock.

Sometimes we appear to be dead, even after we have given our lives to him, and we surely do need a "shot" to get us going again. It is too easy to be lethargic and appear lifeless, but that is not what God desires for our lives. Our Shepherd wants us to thrive and live life to the fullest. Some may pursue the abundant life more diligently than others. But while we have breath our Shepherd does not give up on any of us. Like the "dead lambs," we sometimes find ourselves taking baby steps in the process of becoming mature members of God's flock. He will provide the nourishment and therapy we need to become fully-developed children in his kingdom. He enables us to heal, grow, and become more like him each day. He does all this because he loves us and desires our fellowship. How kind and patient he is!

–Millie

TO PONDER:

• Do I ever feel as though I am spiritually dead? What causes this feeling?

• Is this sense of "deadness" a result of distancing myself from God, or have I ever committed my life to him in the first place?

• How can I reverse this devastating sensation of "being dead in trespasses and sin?"

• Compare the "dead" feeling with the "alive in Christ" feeling. Which would you prefer to have?

TO PRAY:

Holy Shepherd, please forgive me for being content to live as though I am still "dead" in my trespasses and sins. Instead, fill me with your Holy Spirit. Fill my life with a desire to serve and worship only you. Take away the carnal cravings which have ruled my life and show me your will for my life. All glory to you, and you alone!

34
Not Our Final Home

All these people were still living by faith when they died. They did not receive the things promised; they only saw them and welcomed them from a distance, admitting that they were foreigners and strangers on earth. People who say such things show that they are looking for a country of their own. If they had been thinking of the country they had left, they would have had opportunity to return. Instead, they were longing for a better country—a heavenly one. Therefore God is not ashamed to be called their God, for he has prepared a city for them.

–Hebrews 11:13-16 (NIV)

No one who has lived for any time on this earth ever said life is fair.

The ewe had a set of twins, one ewe, one ram. Both were alert and hungry. Both had managed to get up and were beginning to look for their first meal outside the womb when it became clear that something was very wrong. The perky little ewe lamb stood up and was wagging her little tail vigorously but she only stood on three legs. The fourth leg was there, but it dangled uselessly. The mother had given birth to about a dozen lambs previously, none with any sort of problem. It was "just one of those things."

The leg was not broken. If so, I could have splinted it, and it would likely have healed. Perhaps some trauma during the five months the lamb was in her mother's uterus had caused the blood flow to be cut off from the leg, rendering the appendage dead and useless. Even worse, the little ewe had to hop to keep it from dragging on the ground. I thought about trying to construct a prosthesis for her, but there was nothing to attach it to, and doing so was beyond my ability. Initially, when I saw the three-legged baby, I thought the best thing was to humanely put her down, but she got up nearly as quickly as her twin. She had a lot of heart, and her mother seemed patient with the little lamb, so I decided to wait and see.

The three-legged lamb did amazingly well. She didn't appear to be missing any meals. She moved well, hopping on her three legs. In the pen, she either lay beside her twin and mother or, as she got older, would join the other lambs.

When she was about three months old, I weaned her along with the other lambs of my flock. Again, she was able to get to the feeder and waterer and in and out of the barn with no problem. As she grew heavier in body, she labored more in her movements. She rested more than the other lambs. But her balance was amazing.

Then the late spring day came when I let the lambs out to graze on the pasture. At first the flock of lambs was hesitant to venture far from the pen. First, the lambs nibbled at the green blades of grass near the pen, returning often to the security of the barn. Over the next couple of weeks, the lambs grew more confident and ventured farther and farther into the pasture. Since sheep are unable to outrun, kick, or bite a predator, they frequently run back into the pen at the slightest provocation. Their sensitivity to danger is extreme. Something as benign as a jack rabbit sprinting from one hiding place to another may cause the flock to sprint back to the safety of the barn.

The three-legged ewe lamb could not keep up with the flock when they ran back to the barn. As the rest of the lambs grew, they became faster; but as the three-legged ewe lamb grew, the extra weight slowed her down.

Mornings, when I opened the gate for the lambs to go out to pasture, she would try to run with them, but was soon outdistanced. Fear of being alone in the pasture caused her to turn around and come back to the barn. Eventually, she quit leaving the pen with the other lambs. She looked longingly at the green grass as her corral mates ran out to pasture. She wanted to join them; but past experience told her she didn't dare.

I made sure she had hay to eat in place of the pasture she missed, but it seemed her little sheep heart was hurt and confused. She longed for what she could not have, for what she would never have. A few days later I made an appointment to have her harvested at the processing plant where I take all my lambs. They practice humane slaughter, and the meat goes to nourish my wonderful customers. The three-legged ewe lamb and those born with four legs, met the same end; but, somehow, it was harder to deliver her to the plant than the others. At least her suffering was over.

This little ewe's longing for something she would never have reminds me of humankind's earthly existence. There are times of joy and delight, but satisfaction from external sources is fleeting. The homecoming is not quite as joyous as we anticipated. The vacation is over too quickly. People we depend on inevitably disappoint us. Heartbreaking disillusionment can lead to depression, self mutilation, violence, even suicide.

We know one of the many names of God is The One Who Sees. He sees and feels all my pain. I am comforted to read in Revelation 21:4 that when this earth has passed away and we enter heaven, God himself will wipe away every tear. There will be no more sorrow or crying or pain.

Earth is not our final home. Every person intuitively knows there has to be more than the ten, fifty, or eighty years a person may spend on this earth. Hebrews chapter 11 confirms what we all know: This earth is not all there is! There is a home that will give us complete satisfaction, but we cannot live in our new home until we leave this earth, and then only if we have chosen to follow the Good Shepherd. When we have made that choice, we will gaze toward and long for the green pastures of our heavenly home being prepared for us.

–Marilyn

To Ponder:

- Is it encouraging or discouraging to know that the "greats" of the Bible, like Abel, Abraham, and Noah did not receive the things promised to them while on earth?
- What are some unfair realities of this world with which I struggle?
- How does understanding this world as only a temporary home change my daily priorities?

To Pray:

Good Shepherd, help me trust that you understand the evil and discouragement of living on planet earth, and that you love me deeply. You feel my pain and will lead me to my ultimate home. Give me the same attitude you had when you lived on earth among sinful, disappointing people. Let me not become discouraged, but let the reality of this earth as temporary urge me to seek your priorities for my life. Give me courage to run the race you have set before me.

Sheep are mentioned more than 500 times in the Bible.

35
Green Pastures

The Lord is my shepherd; I shall not want. He makes me to lie down in green pastures; He leads me beside the still waters. He restores my soul; He leads me in the paths of righteousness for His name's sake.

–Psalm 23:1-3 (NKJV)

"Diet time," I called as I walked into the barnyard on a biting cold, early-winter morning. "Your corn diet ends today."

The ewes had heard me coming and were already gathered at the gate, expecting to rush out and eat the delectable kernels they love so much. "You're not going to be happy about this, but I can't have you pregnant ladies gaining too much weight."

During one breeding period three years ago, I had fed grain to the ewes throughout their gestation. The lambs were born strong but huge. Half of them I had to pull through the birth canal. Normally, less than ten percent of ewes need birthing assistance.

"I'll not stress you again by feeding you so much corn, even though I know how much you like it." My ewes were not understanding or appreciating this break from routine.

The ewes continued to baa at me, insisting I open the gate, so they could run out and eat the high-carbohydrate yellow kernels. Instead, I opened the other gate for them to enter the hay storage area.

I threw leafy chunks of alfalfa hay into their feeder.

"Here you go, ladies."

A few of the ewes came to the feeder to nibble hay then left in a huff, as if to say, "Hey, come on, that's not what we eat first thing in the morning!"

In a sheep's world, I would compare corn to a human eating bacon, cookies, or chocolate. There is high palatability, yet limited nutrition. Corn provides sheep with calories and energy, yet has little protein or vitamins and minerals. Just as we can certainly enjoy bacon, cookies or chocolate in moderation, most of us don't need high-calorie, low-nutrient food. This is how I view feeding corn to my sheep.

Typically, I will feed the ewes some corn during breeding season to increase the chance of twins over singles. During lactation, I feed a little corn to provide the extra energy. And, when customers request it, I finish some meat lambs with corn added to their hay.

My opinion that corn should be minimized in a feeding program is a minority view, but my study of corn and other grains shows it to be inflammatory and marginal nutritionally, so I have chosen to limit it. I want all or most of my sheep's diet to be pasture grass and hay.

I also decline to feed my sheep fish meal, blood meal, and bone meal—all great sources of protein that are popular feed supplements, particularly for lambs raised for the show ring. In my view, sheep are herbivores, so I promote a protocol that excludes any category of animal protein.

My woolies object with gusto when I feed corn then cease feeding corn. They love it as much as I love chocolate. However, if they never eat corn, they don't miss it. It is the withdrawal from corn that leaves them craving it. While they are eating corn, they never seem to be satisfied, always desiring more. The shepherd who feeds grain must take care to store the grain so that his sheep will not help themselves to it. If sheep get access to a large quantity of grain, most will eat with abandon, some to the point of death, because an over abundance causes extreme toxicity in the digestive parts.

Good pasture, in my opinion, is the very best feed for sheep. When the pasture is abundant and green, the sheep love grazing and return with full, satisfied bellies. They would actually rather stay in and eat hay, because it is less work. However, once they are forced out onto a quality pasture, they gain weight and become fit and healthy.

Pasture offers a variety of plants, which gives them a variety of nutrients. Studies have shown that animals will actually seek out plants containing nutrients they are lacking. When sheep are fed hay in feed bunks, as mine are in winter, they fight for the best bits of hay. The younger and larger ones push away the weaker animals. Pasture is different. The weaker and smaller animals have just as much opportunity to eat and fill their bellies as the stronger, more aggressive sheep.

When a sheep lies down in a green pasture, this is because it is satisfied. The imagery in the Shepherd's Psalm was very clear to the people of King David's time. When the Lord is a person's shepherd, there is complete satisfaction. The follower's path is clear and the soul is at peace.

How often do we, like sheep seeking more and more corn, run after the pleasures of the world to satisfy our souls? I think we also view God's blessings as limited. Like the sheep fighting over a feeding of hay, we fight to acquire the things—whether material things, entertainment, popularity, or something else we think will make us happy. The problem is, things of the world will never satisfy our souls. We were created to be satisfied only by a relationship with the Great Shepherd and to find soul rest only in his green pastures.

Until I was in my late twenties, I loved to shop. Of

course I understand that we must shop in our modern society. In my youth, though, I was driven to buy the things I felt I had missed out on during an austere upbringing. My parents had tried to instill in me frugality, to save for a rainy day, to under-spend so I could be generous toward others.

Once I surrendered my materialism to the Good Shepherd, I felt content with what I had. I still occasionally enjoy a shopping trip when I am truly in need, but otherwise I am content to stay away from the malls. I know that for some people, materialism is an ongoing struggle.

Today there are so many poor substitutes for godly contentment, including social media, Ipods loaded with favorite music, television, novels, social engagements. The list goes on.

Just recently, I realized I had put another idol before God. When I exercised or did outside chores, I liked to listen to audio books. One day I was preparing to go outside to work, and I realized I didn't have an audio book. Something akin to panic jolted me. At that moment I felt the Lord speak to my spirit, "Marilyn, would you really prefer to listen to another so-so book over communing with the God of the Universe?"

Gulp. I don't want to imply that appropriate media is bad, and I will probably return to listening to audio books when and if the Lord releases me to do that. In the meantime, while I weed the garden or clean stalls, I am enjoying just hanging out with God, conversing with him as he restores my soul.

–Marilyn

To Ponder:

- How am I seeking to fill the void that only a relationship with the Great Shepherd can fill?
- Is it possible even good things, such as service to others or keeping my body fit, are interfering with a wholehearted pursuit of my Shepherd?

To Pray:

Thank you, Good Shepherd, for offering me absolutely everything I need to satisfy my soul. Let me say "no" to the deceiver, who is lying about temporal things having eternal importance. Encourage me to seek your satisfying green pastures and find rest for my soul. Help me, as I live in *the world, not to be* of *the world. Teach me to enjoy fellowship with you. Lead me beside still waters. Restore my soul.*

36
The Record Books

And I saw the dead, small and great, standing before God, and the books were opened. And another book was opened, which is the Book of Life. And the dead were judged according to their works, by the things which were written in the books.

–Revelation 20:12 (NKJV)

Lightning danced across the sky, in sync with the roars of nearing thunder.

"Hurry up, Shel; we don't want to get caught in a downpour or hit by lightning," I shouted above the bellow of the nearing storm. We broke into a run for the barn. It was time to "work" the newest lambs in the jugs.

As we entered the lambing barn, the darkness enveloped us like a black cloud until I hit the light switch. As we moved from pen to pen, catching each lamb, we took turns banding and ear tagging each one. I held the record book, making sure all the facts were correctly recorded for each new baby. By the time we finished, the thunderstorm had moved on. We slowly strolled back to the house, chatting about our plans for this crop of lambs.

A few weeks ago, I rounded up all the record books that I have kept since I started raising sheep. What memories it brought back as I browsed through each one. Every year at lambing time, every ewe was recorded as she gave birth. Recorded was her name and number in the left column, her babies' numbers, then a notation of their sex in the right column. If the lamb was a male, his ear tag was usually blue or green, and the females sported orange, red, or yellow ear tags. This simplified the task, when needed, of choosing a specific sex at a distance. Then in the middle column, was the date and time of day the ewe lambed, and whether she presented us with a single, twins, or triplets. A few times quadruplets appeared.

Just for fun, I sometimes included the outside temperature at the time of the birth. For example, an entry on February 1, 1985 at 6:00 a.m. noted a temperature of minus twenty-seven degrees. That whole lambing season was unusually cold! No wonder our electricity bill escalated with all the "heat lamps" plugged in to keep those babies from freezing.

During lambing, I checked the ewes multiple times day and night. When it was exceptionally cold, I checked as often as every two hours. There have been times I just waited for a ewe to give birth before going back to bed. Sometimes to speed things up, if the birth was imminent, I went ahead and pulled the lambs and made sure they ate and were doing well before I left.

It is satisfying to recall the different sheep that became special friends to me. These sheep usually had a name and, sometimes, a number. The books also recorded the health problems, delivery problems, deaths and outcomes in the life of each sheep that lived in my flock. There are records of the sale of each lamb, its weight, the price received, and names of purchasers.

The records even reveal the production of each ewe. Those who didn't "pay their way" were culled, or sold, and had their names in my record book blotted out. Not all results were happy, and it broke my heart to lose, or need to cull, a favorite ewe.

I also discovered the original plans drawn for my new

lambing barn back when we built the new house just up the road from the original homestead. It was exciting to be able to set up individual pens, or jugs, in my new barn in anticipation of welcoming all those new babies. Here they could be born, put under heat lamps to dry off, and get acquainted with their moms and siblings. It was great to have the ewes and babies out of the bad weather, safe from predators and free to eat without competition from other sheep.

How important it is to keep records! Even God keeps records of all humanity. Like the sheep record books, the Lord knows each of us by name, and he knows everything about us. He keeps record of all our deeds, whether good or bad, and he knows the good acts that were done in his name. He recalls which of our works were for self aggrandizement, and which were done to bring glory to him. Our heavenly Shepherd even knows exactly when we decided to become his child, a member of his flock. He knows when someone is struggling to give their heart to the Lord; he is patient and will wait, providing encouragement through his human shepherds.

Not only does our heavenly Shepherd know all about us, he is preparing a perfect place for us to spend eternity. He promised in John 14:1-4 that he was going to prepare a place for us that we may live with him forever. We know that place as Heaven. There we will find a perfect home.

Revelation chapter 20 teaches us that each person will appear at the throne of judgment. When the Book of Life is opened, those whose names are not written there will be judged according to the sinfulness of their deeds and cast into "the lake of fire" (Rev. 20:14).

Those whose names are written in the Book of Life will be rewarded according to the motives of their hearts and the faith in which they lived their lives. Deeds not done for Christ will be burned up as hay, wood, and stubble (I Corinthians 3:13).

However, good deeds do not give us salvation from sin and eternal life. Only when we repent and receive Christ as Savior is our sin erased and our name written in the Book of Life. I want my name to be found there. Don't you?

–Millie

To Ponder:

- Is there any way I can hide anything from God?
- Is my name written in the Book of Life? If not, what do I need to do to get my name there?
- Am I looking forward to spending eternity in Heaven with my Shepherd? Or do I have doubts about my salvation? How can I receive assurance?

To Pray:

Dear Heavenly Shepherd, I am thankful you know all about me and have promised to wipe away all my sins when I ask for forgiveness. Thank-you for preparing a beautiful home where I will spend eternity with you and all your other sheep, including my believing family and friends. Give me courage to lead others to this knowledge, so they can be assured of eternity in Heaven, also.

37
Don't Blame the Shepherd

Nevertheless we, according to His promise, look for new heavens and a new earth in which righteousness dwells. Therefore, beloved, looking forward to these things, be diligent to be found by Him in peace, without spot and blameless.

–II Peter 3:13-14 (NKJV)

Accidents can happen when dealing with livestock. Sometimes the result is downright tragic. Several years ago we were speaking with an acquaintance when he mentioned, "My granddaughter decided to join 4-H with a sheep project. We bought a ewe lamb and would like to get her bred. Would it be possible to bring her to "visit" your ram?"

It was not an unusual request as we frequently obliged members of 4-H (a youth group who raise and exhibit various projects) or F.F.A (Future Farmers of America). Few of the kids own their own ram, as it's not financially feasible to purchase one for just a handful of ewes. So we were frequently asked for the use of ours. We responded to the grandfather, "Sure, Bill, that would be fine. You'll get a beautiful lamb from him. Bring her over."

The nice-looking ewe lamb arrived and was immediately placed in the corral with the rest of our sheep herd. All went well for a few days and the newly-introduced ewe seemed to have no issues with the unfamiliar sheep in her new environment.

One morning when I went out to do the chores, things seemed to be in an uproar. As I entered the shed, I found the young "visiting ewe" caught in the wire panel that served as a wall of the corral. She had apparently decided to see what was on the other side of the fence. In her attempt to leap over the panel, her hind leg went through the wire in such a way that it was "woven" back and forth, tightly gripped by the unforgiving structure of the panel. Each place the leg was pressed against the wire, the flesh had been gashed clear to the bone as she fought for hours to free herself. We cut the wire in several places to release her, and the leg just dangled back and forth. We knew the ewe's leg was beyond repair, so we called Bill and explained the situation. Fortunately, he was very understanding and didn't blame us. "These things happen," he said. "It wasn't your fault; there was nothing you could do about it."

Bill called a veterinarian who, after examining the lamb, recommended she be "put down." The damage was just too extensive, and the leg would never fully heal. I felt really bad and blamed myself; I should have had a higher fence over which the little ewe would not have attempted to jump. But the owner didn't hold it against me and actually apologized for putting us to the trouble. He could have gotten angry and threatened to sue us, but he was forgiving and not blaming. All was not lost since they butchered the lamb and enjoyed the meat for their table.

When our girls were young, sometimes one of them was designated to "check the sheep," usually after school when I needed to be gone. Occasionally, there would be a dead lamb or some other problem. It was a spontaneous reaction to blame that girl if she forgot, or was late, in checking. In these situations, often valuable lessons are learned, and the negligence rarely occurred again. However, when I had to reprimand a daughter, she inevitably tried to put the blame on someone, or something, else. Often my husband and I heard the words, "Don't blame me; it wasn't me."

Why do we find it so hard to take the blame ourselves? It is difficult not to place the blame on someone else when an egregious action occurs, but we are never too old to learn the valuable lesson of owning up to our own mistakes.

It is common to hear someone say they won't go to a church because churches are full of hypocrites. Jesus said he came to heal the sick. The church is full of "the sick;" what better place for them to go? If everyone was "well," there wouldn't be much need for a church. There are those who refuse to attend a certain church because a particular person goes there, or perhaps they don't like the preacher because what he says "is not what I need." The excuses are countless.

It is important to remember that humankind's blame game is a way of avoiding truth. Blaming others instead of accepting blame for oneself is an act of immaturity. As we grow emotionally and spiritually, it is important that we learn to not only accept blame, we also need to forgive and make right the wrongs we have wrought through our negative behavior.

The only human who was ever truly blameless was our wonderful Shepherd, Jesus Christ. At Calvary, Christ took the penalty for our sin, offering us forgiveness and cleansing. But while we walk this earth, we must make choices, we may often make mistakes, and we must guard against sin.

What a glorious promise our Shepherd left us when he told us to look for new heavens and a new earth where righteousness will dwell. As we look forward to these things, let us strive to live in peace, without spot and blameless—a constant challenge.

–Millie

To Ponder:

- Do I find it easy to place the blame on someone or something else for my own mistakes and sins? Why is this so?
- Will we be blaming others in Heaven? Assuming the answer is "no," why not start now to quit the blame game?
- Since Christ has forgiven me, what should be my attitude toward the offenses of others?

To Pray:

Heavenly Shepherd, thank you that I will be found blameless in the new heavens and the new earth. Forgive me for the times I deserved the blame but shoved it off on someone else. I am excited for that day when you will reign as King over all in a kingdom of tranquility.

Sometimes we get glimpses of the peaceable kingdom where "the wolf will live with the lamb, the leopard will lie down with the goat, and the calf and the lion and the yearling together" (Isaiah 11:6-7, NIV).

38
Think On These Things

Finally, brethren, whatever things are true, whatever things are noble, whatever things are just, whatever things are pure, whatever things are lovely, whatever things are of good report, if there is any virtue and if there is anything praiseworthy—meditate on these things.

–Philippians 4:8 (NKJV)

"Girls, come quickly! The sheep are in the alfalfa." Mom's urgent shout from the back door broke the tranquility of the hot afternoon.

"Coming," I yelled, running down the creaky stairs of our old farmhouse, my two younger sisters on my heels.

Sheep and fresh alfalfa—not a good combination. We had been instructed over and over again not to let the sheep get into the alfalfa field any time before a hard freeze. Sheep love the green, lush legume grown by many farmers during summer. It is cut, baled, and fed as hay throughout the year. However, when sheep eat a lot of fresh alfalfa in a short amount of time, they experience a tremendous buildup of gas.

"They will bloat really fast," Mom and Dad had warned. When we asked why, Dad had explained that because sheep have multi-chambered stomachs, digestion is complex, taking three times the amount of time digestion takes for non-ruminant animals like pigs or horses. Therefore, the bloating associated with gas buildup is magnified in their complex digestive systems.

As we rushed out toward the alfalfa field, we saw most of the flock eating the rich green leaves with gusto. I imagine, for them, eating unfettered in that lush alfalfa field was like me finding myself in a chocolate factory, allowed to eat without restriction.

"Get back in the pen." My sister yelled, running full speed toward the placid ewes. "Don't you know that could kill you?" She screamed. We all shooed them back into the pen. Despite the perilous situation, even as the ewes ambled back toward the corral, they sneaked bites of alfalfa.

Chasing the last of the escapees back into their pen, we found that a few of the ewes already had huge sides, as if each ewe had swallowed two volleyballs, one protruding from either side. Several of the ewes began to labor in their breathing. A few dropped to their knees.

"Marilyn, get that piece of garden hose from the barn." Mom's voice was confident but urgent, prompting me to run in search of the hose. When I returned with the hose, Dad straddled between his knees one of the ewes that had gone down. He pulled her neck and head forward. Together my parents threaded the hose piece down the throat of the downed ewe. When instructed, my sisters and I pushed on the ewe's sides to expel the gas and chewed alfalfa. It smelled like vegetables left too long in the bottom of a refrigerator. We turned our heads and held our breath, making faces at each other.

"I think that is the best we can do for her." When no more gas or crushed alfalfa emerged, my mom pulled the hose piece out of the ewe's throat. She pointed at another sheep that was down on her belly and laboring to breathe. "Grab that ewe."

The first ewe we had hosed seemed to be breathing better and was back on her feet, but the second one didn't get up when we pulled the hose out. "Marilyn, run into the kitchen and get one of my long-bladed knives." Panic was rising in Mom's voice.

Knife, I thought, as I rushed to the house. *Why a knife?*

"Give me the knife," said Dad. He had specs of smelly, green alfalfa splattered on his shirt and hands. "This ewe will die if we don't release the gas." He plunged the knife into the bulging left side of a downed ewe. "She may die anyway, but we have to try." Dad pulled out the knife and voluminous, putrid liquid grass spewed out of the ewe's side. "This area here on the left side is where the stomach is closest to the surface of the skin." He instructed us, as we covered our noses.

Bloat is a fast-moving malady, but my parents' knowledge and ability to act quickly saved a lot of our ewes. Three of the forty-some ewes that participated in the alfalfa escapade died. We had to disinfect and stitch up the ewes with holes in their sides. At the time, it seemed a disaster; but in reality, we were fortunate no more died. The surviving ewes had pretty sore tummies for several days after their venture into the alfalfa field. We fixed and reinforced the fence where they had escaped.

The crazy thing is, given the opportunity, the majority of our flock would run right back to the alfalfa field, once their tummies healed. But before we come down too hard on sheep, let us consider that human decisions can be just as self-destructive and irrational. Alcoholics who have lost their families and jobs keep on drinking. Many meth addicts have lost the same, plus their teeth and twenty years of their lives, but they still live to get their meth high.

It's not only addicts and lawbreakers who choose to feast on things that are not beneficial to them. People can become addicted to their electronics, whether television, a smart phone, or a Facebook account. Some are so consumed with their hobbies, that it overtakes their work and family time.

And—now I'm really going to step on some toes—some are so obsessed with presenting a clean house at all times, at any cost, that a perfectly-kept home becomes more important than relationships.

There is nothing inherently wrong with electronics, hobbies, or keeping a clean house. The problem is when we become obsessed with anything to the point it overtakes us.

Our Great Shepherd tells us to focus on things that are true, noble, pure and good. He knows that when we meditate and set our minds on these things, his priorities will prevail. Over-indulging in anything may become harmful to our lives, whether physical, mental, spiritual or social. Only when we place the Lord's priorities in the forefront will we find true peace and satisfaction. And, yes, a little chocolate is OK.

–Marilyn

To Ponder:

- What socially good and acceptable things in my life are distracting me from the Good Shepherd's priorities?
- How can I "think on these things," keep my mind on what is good and true and pure?
- What changes need I make to put things I enjoy in their proper place, rather than allowing them to overtake God's priorities for my life?

To Pray:

Thank you, Jesus, my Good Shepherd, that my faith is not a list of things I must and must not do; rather it is a relationship with you, the God of the Universe. Let me not become caught up in things I should or should not be doing; but let me be led by the Holy Spirit to spend time and energy on the priorities you alone know are best for me. I ask you to guide my decisions, so that what I am doing and who I am becoming may glorify you.

Lambs are social and love to eat and play together.

39
Don't Be Discouraged

We are hard pressed on every side, yet not crushed; we are perplexed, but not in despair.... Therefore, we do not lose heart. Even though our outward man is perishing, yet the inward man is being renewed day by day.

–II Corinthians 4:8, 16 (NKJV)

Little Timmy was the runt, the smallest baby in a set of triplets. But his heart was as huge as his body was small, and he tried to do everything that the bigger lambs did. At feeding time when the ewes were eating their hay, all the lambs played "follow the leader," racing from one end of the corral to the opposite side. Of course, Timmy ran with them but, being so tiny, he was always way behind the crowd. When they ran, the noise of so many feet pounding across the corral sounded like a thunderstorm threatening.

Timmy's constant baaing sounded like, "Wait for me, slow down." But he complained to no avail. Although he scurried as fast as his short legs could carry him, he lagged farther and farther behind.

As the leading lambs reached the fence, in one accord they spun around for the return trip across the pen. Without fail, Timmy was, once again, mowed down by his larger siblings. But as soon as the wave of lambs had passed over him, he hopped up, and in good spirits shook himself and sped after the others. He never gave up even though they never waited for him, never checked to see if he was hurt, and tromped over him when he was down. Eventually, Timmy grew up as large as the other lambs. His days of being wiped out were over, and he could finally keep up with the flock.

If only we were as persistent in our faith as Timmy was in his desire to run with the herd of lambs. We strive to be obedient to God, but it is so difficult to keep on track, and oh, how easy it is to become discouraged and give up. We may compare ourselves with a vibrant Christian leader who has many spiritual gifts and appears to have it "all together." Perhaps we try to imitate a well-known speaker, a popular singer, or someone else with character strengths and gifts we admire, but it becomes a fruitless venture. Our sovereign Shepherd does provide what we need, but not always what we want. Don't be discouraged! If God gives you assurance you are in his will, then get up, shake off the feeling of incompetence, and try again.

There are times we feel as if a friend has failed us. Perhaps they have told an untruth or exaggerated the truth about us, to make us appear untrustworthy. We need to approach that friend and confront them, giving them opportunity to make things right. Offer your forgiveness and, like Timmy, shake it off. Do not share the injustice with others! Get up and get going again.

If we are obedient to God, we can't fail, although it may seem like we do. The Lord may have a different plan for us. Sometimes we try to accomplish our desires by ourselves rather than trusting God to guide us. What we want to do is not always God's plan. Our ambitions need to be bathed in prayer and left in God's hands. It is through our own efforts that we try to keep up with the crowd. The Lord doesn't care if we "keep up." He just wants our trust and obedience. God has promised he will be there to help us, and we can overcome discouragement if we allow him to be our guide.

I want to be as persistent as Timmy and never allow myself to become depressed and discouraged.

–Millie

To Ponder:

- Is feeling trampled on a result of the actions of others or myself?
- How can I rid myself of these discouraging feelings?
- How can I trust God and allow him to work in and through me, rather than try to take care of problems myself?
- Have I ever been accused falsely by a friend? How was the conflict resolved? Was it a successful resolution?

To Pray:

Heavenly Father, thank you for being my Shepherd and for loving me so much. I am sorry for the times I fall and feel trampled on. Please help me obey you, get back up, forgive others, and look to you for encouragement. Give me the patience, wisdom, and graciousness I need when dealing with someone who has wounded me. Show me how I can do your will and follow your instructions. Please renew my inner person every day.

40
It's All About the Smell

But thanks be to God, who always leads us as captives in Christ's triumphal procession and uses us to spread the aroma of the knowledge of him everywhere. For we are to God the pleasing aroma of Christ among those who are being saved and those who are perishing. To the one we are an aroma that brings death; to the other, an aroma that brings life. And who is equal to such a task?

–II Corinthians 2:14-16 (NIV)

"Oh no, I was worried you would do that." I stood in the lambing pen of the Suffolk ewe that gave birth to triplets the previous afternoon. "Can't quite feed all three, huh, girl?"

Earlier in the day I had noticed the black-faced ewe with big, floppy ears push away her smallest lamb. "Well, let's see if we can't convince your mama to keep you." I spoke with conviction I did not feel. The lamb bleated and wagged his tail, anticipating mid-morning snack. "I'm going to get a halter and tie up your mama, so she has to stand still." I did as promised, preventing the new mother from pushing away the smallest of her babies. Instead, she stomped her foot and kicked when I pushed her lamb back toward her udder to nurse.

"This is not looking good for you, little one." As if in response, he baaed and nibbled on my sweatshirt hood strings.

A few hours later when I checked the triplets and their mother, the ewe butted the small lamb hard, flipping him up and into her water bucket. "That is enough!" I told her, although I knew this was nature's way of pushing off a weak lamb when a ewe was unable to feed all her babies. Still, it broke my heart to see a ewe, who had licked off all her newborns and protected them when they first walked on their wobbly little legs, become aggressive against one of them.

I put the small triplet in its own pen, not looking forward to the extra work and expense of bottle-feeding; but otherwise, he would die.

"Maybe, just maybe we can get you a new mama." I stroked the lamb's silky black face and head and rubbed his kinky lamb-wool coat. "Not likely, but we'll see."

I knew that when it comes to grafting an orphan lamb onto a new ewe, it is all about the smell. I don't know biologically why this is so; however, what I observe over and over is that when the ewe licks off a lamb, she apparently absorbs the unique odor of the lamb or perhaps the ewe's own odor is transferred to the lamb. I also know that smell is the primary means by which the ewe will identify her lambs throughout their lives. When lambs come running to Mama at mealtime, she sniffs their rumps to ensure they really are her lambs. If they pass the sniff test, they eat. If not, they get an aggressive butt from the ewe, discouraging them from trying again.

I continued to feed the lamb with a bottle made from powdered, lamb's milk. Several days later, a ewe gave birth to a single. Now was my chance. As soon as her lamb was born, I took the expelled placenta or afterbirth and rubbed it all over the orphan lamb. I knew it was not likely I would be able to convince the new mother that the four-day-old lamb was hers, but I hoped the smell of the afterbirth from her own lamb would be enough to convince the new mother to adopt the orphan as her own.

"There you go, girl. I'm pretty sure you can feed them both." I put both lambs—the older orphan and her own newborn—under her nose. "Looks like you are saying, 'I only remember giving birth to one lamb; what's this?'"

The ewe sniffed and snorted. When the orphan lamb realized the potential, he jumped up and went for the new mother's udder. She promptly butted him away. "Oh no, here we go, again. Sorry, little guy."

I tried for over a day to get this ewe to accept the orphan. She was adamant that she had only one lamb, and eventually, for his own safety and because he wasn't able to drink from the ewe anyway, I removed him and resigned myself to having him as a bottle baby. This ewe was able to distinguish the baby born to her from the orphan by their distinctive smells. It is a smell that people cannot differentiate; but ewes can.

The following year, we hosted a young man from Northern Ireland. Rodger was a shepherd visiting the United States on the International Four-H Youth Exchange. His U.S. city hosts knew he wanted to spend some time on a sheep farm, and we were glad to have him in our home for part of his stay.

Wise beyond his nineteen years, Rodger was hard-working, knowledgeable and unassuming. He and I discussed many aspects of sheep raising, including grafting lambs onto adoptive mothers. I shared with him my frustration at rarely being able to graft an older orphan onto another ewe. Rodger shared with me his method for doing this. He takes the afterbirth from the potential adoptive mother, places it in a pan, and fills the pan with lukewarm water. He then takes the lamb to be grafted and puts it into the pan of afterbirth and water. Rodger stressed the importance of swirling the water all over the lamb, including its head, neck and ears, so that the smell of the ewe penetrates the entire surface area of the lamb. It is not a pleasant or clean process, but he claims it is very effective.

Based on what I know about how ewes identify their lambs, this method makes a lot of sense. Rodger's emphasis on total immersion of the orphan lamb into the scent of the potential mother, made me think about this scripture in II Corinthians, which tells us that as Christians we are to be immersed in the "scent" of Christ. That scent is one that is unbelievably pleasing to God. It is a scent we cannot buy and apply. We cannot pretend to have the scent. Either an individual is a believer and gives off the aroma of God, or a person is not a believer and has no such odor.

Of course, "aroma" is figurative. We have all met people that we immediately just knew where they stood spiritually. They wear the Good Shepherd's aroma. God's compassion for others can only emanate from me when I am completely submerged in his grace and love.

I have seen lamb-grafting sprays in sheep-supply catalogs and have even tried some of these products. The spray is applied over the rump and tail area of the orphan lamb and on the nose of the ewe. The principle upon which this product is promoted is that the spray masks the natural odors of both the lamb and the ewe, providing a new, unified odor. Other shepherds may have had success with these sprays; but I do not know anyone who has. The odor is artificial and only temporarily changes the smell on a limited area of the lamb and ewe.

To be genuine in the aroma of Christ, we must be completely submerged in Christ. Those around us will notice his aroma because it is genuine and lasting.

–Marilyn

To Ponder:

- Think of people who are "bathed in the aroma of Christ." How do they affect the people around them?
- What aroma do I emit?
- How can I know I am bathed in the aroma of Christ and emitting this aroma to those whose lives I touch?

To Pray:

Loving and gracious Shepherd, bathe me in your aroma. I want to give off that scent to everyone with whom I come in contact, not for my popularity but for your glory. Let me never be fake or contrived in my love for you or in my love and concern for those you put in my path each day. Let me live my life bathed in your love and grace, so I may extend this same love and grace to others.

Carla feeding one of the many lambs she gave birth to and raised.

41
Carla's Hiding Place

The Lord is my light and my salvation—whom shall I fear? The Lord is the stronghold of my life—of whom shall I be afraid?. . . . . For in the day of trouble he will keep me safe in his dwelling; he will hide me in the shelter of his sacred tent and set me high upon a rock.

–Psalm 27:1, 5 (NIV)

"Carla!" I called for the gentle ewe approaching her eleventh year of life, ancient by the standards of sheep longevity. "Where are you, girl?" We had owned Carla since she was three, and she had given us lambs, usually twins, every year with no problems. She was a good mom and had plenty of milk for her babies . . . until she turned ten. She began having a bit of trouble feeding her twins, so I checked her mouth and found her front teeth ground to the gum.

"It's almost dark and the coyotes will be out soon. I need you to come into the pen for the night, you good old girl."

Since discovering Carla's dental condition, I had called her in from the flock each morning to give her extra leafy hay. She was small and crippled, causing her to come out on the losing end when she had to compete with the other sheep for food. The leafy hay was higher in protein and easier to chew without front teeth. Sometimes she stood on three legs, her front right foot raised, indicating that standing on it hurt her. It was probably arthritis, not uncommon in older farm animals. There was nothing I could do except make her as comfortable as possible. I would have to cull or sell her before the next breeding season. I hated to face that reality. She was such a sweetie, but I operated a commercial farm, not a petting zoo. And it would be inhumane to let her go through another pregnancy with her painful arthritis.

I had weaned all the lambs, including Carla's twins, in early summer. Even without having to feed lambs, Carla remained skinny when I put her back with the ewe flock. She was now in the habit of coming for extra feed, and she would stand at the gate and look at me with her big, soft eyes, little ears perked forward as if waiting for me to say, "OK, Carla, here's your hay."

My concern for Carla that summer evening drove me to search for her with greater urgency as the sun sank closer to the horizon.

Each summer morning, I had let her out into the barnyard where she could eat free choice from the haystack. Where was that cute, toddling little Southdown ewe that so loved to nibble weeds and eat hay?

She had been so quiet, unassuming, and easy to manage. I began to worry that she may have wandered off and had a stroke, or that something else had prevented her from waiting for me at the barn door as usual. Carla always knew when it was time to go back into the pen. Where was she?

My eye caught a slight movement between the haystack and the fence. It was she.

"There you are, Carla! You scared me, old girl, but I see you are happy as can be back there in your own special hideaway."

Carla was stretched out on her belly, chewing her cud, the picture of contentment. It was easy to see she felt protected with the haystack on her one side and the fence on the other.

For the remainder of the summer until I could no longer leave her outside, Carla would go to the place between the fence and the haystack to relax when she finished eating. It was a cool place. The ground was high enough that it was not muddy. Familiar with the nature of sheep, I knew that Carla felt protected in that space between two tall structures. If ever I was unable to find her, I now knew exactly where to look.

Carla looked so satisfied in her special place, that I found myself wishing I, too, had a special hideaway, a place where I would feel comfortable and protected. It then occurred to me that I do have a special place of comfort and protection. It is not a physical structure, but resting in the protection of Jesus, my Good Shepherd, should provide me with complete satisfaction, as Carla's place provided her.

This comfortable place where we are protected is the solace believers can have when they surrender their cares to the Great Shepherd. Like Carla, our sorrows and trials can be many. There is often no healing for our pain on this side of eternity. The woes of humankind are deep and painful, because we live in a fallen world.

While life on this earth is infinitely valuable, it is relatively short. James 4:14 compares our lives to a mist that appears briefly and then is gone. Yet the Good Shepherd, in his great mercy and love, values us. He longs to have us run to him for protection. I hope you also find the Shepherd's place of protection and satisfaction!

–Marilyn

To Ponder:

- Is the temporary aspect of human life on earth, compared to eternity, encouraging or discouraging?
- King David wrote this psalm about safety from enemies and physical danger. What modern-day enemies and dangers threaten us?
- Read the entire text of Psalm 27. What priorities in my life need to be rearranged?

To Pray:

Shepherd of my heart, I praise you that this life is not all there is. Thank you for promising to protect me. Help me remember to run to you when I am fearful. Remind me to always rest in you. Plant eternity in my heart as I daily seek to follow you. At the same time, let me not be so heavenly minded that I am of no earthly good. Keep me mindful of arranging my priorities to glorify you and store up treasures that cannot be destroyed by this world.

42
SUBMISSION: NOW OR LATER?

Therefore submit yourselves to every ordinance of man for the LORD's sake, whether to the king as supreme, or to governors, as to those who are sent by Him for the punishment of evil-doers and for the praise of those who do good. For this is the will of God, that by doing good you may put to silence the ignorance of foolish men.

–I Peter 2:13-15 (NKJV)

"Jim, Jim, what am I going to do with you? You are going to get eaten if you keep running off from the flock."

Jim, the lamb, was frustrating the shepherd to no end. The sheep herder was in charge of a huge band of sheep in the hills which teemed with wildlife, including bears, lions, wolves, eagles and other predators. Jim, a young lamb with a wanderlust spirit, refused to stay with the band of sheep which the sheepherder and his dog kept tightly contained. This was the only way of protecting the grazing sheep.

The herder continued to scold Jim. "Just last week, your buddy strayed from the security of the flock. Don't you recall when the big bear snuck up on him and grabbed him, carrying him off for dinner?" It was a fairly common occurrence for a bear, wolf, or mountain lion to visit the sheep camp, looking for an opportunity to nab a tasty lamb.

In large flocks, it is unusual for the shepherd to name a lamb, but this one held a special place in the heart of the shepherd, so Jim acquired a name. This lamb with the independent mind had the rare trait of not wanting to stay near the other sheep. He was exceptionally curious and constantly wandered out of bounds in spite of the shepherd's watchful care. Jim even defied the dog trained to obey the shepherd's commands.

Finally, the sheep herder had no other recourse. He lovingly gathered Jim in his arms and broke his front leg. It hurt Jim, but it also hurt the shepherd, who took such drastic measures because of his fondness for the wayward lamb. Out of love, he had to discipline the lamb who had no idea why his caregiver had hurt him. With a broken front leg, Jim could hop around and eat, but was not able to stray any distance from the other sheep. What a hard lesson!

• • •

"It's your turn to exercise the lambs," our girls argued back and forth."

"No, it's not, I did it last time!" So went the disagreement, night after night.

When our three daughters were young, they were involved in 4-H and FFA, showing sheep at the county fair and other small fairs in the area. They picked out their "fair lambs" when the lambs were very young, and it was quite an ordeal to get those lambs trained for the show.

For weeks, the girls would work with their lambs. First, they had to halter the lambs and tie them up until they quit fighting to escape. Then they led the lambs around and trained them to stand properly as they would need to do in the show ring. All kinds of training methods were involved in teaching the lambs to "brace" for the judge. Bracing, or standing with tightened muscles, made the lambs look attractive and feel firm to the judge's touch. The lamb had to be trained to push back against the girl showing it to achieve a "brace." Each night and morning, the lambs were exercised, the girls running the lambs back and forth over small jumps to firm up their muscles.

As fair day neared, the girls sheared and washed their projects. They trimmed and polished the hooves with black shoe polish, and cleaned out the greasy build-up in the ears. The lambs were then covered with a special "blanket" to keep them clean. Talk about submission! Those lambs surely learned how to submit.

Our Scripture speaks of submission to those in authority. Through our act of submission to our leaders, we are witnesses of Christ—to the leaders as well as to others around us.

Some years ago, I heard about a Christian man who always ran the stop sign at a rural, four-way stop sign. As he approached the stop sign, he would look both ways, and if there was no traffic, or no traffic close to the intersection, he didn't bother to stop. Another man who lived in a house near this corner took notice and was heard to remark that he didn't think a Christian would do that. The stop sign runner's refusal to submit to the rules of the government created a poor witness for the neighbor who didn't understand why a Christian would disobey a traffic rule.

It is imperative that we be cognizant of those around us and how our behavior and attitudes affect our witness to them. Unless the required government order is a blatant violation of our morals and biblical values, we need to obey the rules determined by those in authority over us. In Romans chapter 13, the Apostle Paul admonishes us to be subject to the governing authorities, adding that the Lord has put these authorities in position over us for good and not for evil.

More importantly, we need to submit to the will of God. When we question or rebel against God's will, he disciplines us. You hear of the parent who, when preparing to discipline her child says, "This hurts me as much as it hurts you." Of course, the child doesn't believe it, but I think God has the same feeling when disciplining us. It hurts him to have to punish us, and we often think it is unfair, but our Shepherd knows why he is taking the action. We need to trust him and submit to his loving discipline.

Eventually, each and every one of us will require a submissive spirit when we come face to face with our Creator God. Like my daughters' fair lambs, we can choose to submit; or like Jim the wayward lamb, we can wait until our lives are full of pain and brokenness before we submit.

–Millie

To Ponder:

- Am I willing to submit to the heavenly Shepherd, or do I stubbornly insist on my own way?
- Consider who is included in "those in authority" over us.
- How can discipline be a "growth tool" for me?
- Why does it hurt the heavenly Father when he disciplines his children? What is the best response to his discipline?

To Pray:

Heavenly Shepherd, please forgive me for the times when I have been too stubborn to submit to you. I know you want what is best for me, yet I can't always understand what that is. Give me a submissive attitude. Help me to be discerning and wise in my reactions toward all authorities that are over me in this life. Help me to be a true witness of your presence in my heart and life. Help me remember those around me are watching to see what I will do in each situation. Thank you for your awesome love and faithfulness. Thank you for holding me in your arms even as you are disciplining me, Good Shepherd.

A crossbred ewe and lamb

43
Eternity In Our Hearts

He has made everything beautiful in its time. He has also set eternity in the human heart; yet no one can fathom what God has done from beginning to end.

–Ecclesiastes 3:11 (NIV)

At age nine I joined the Box Elder 4-H Club in Kersey, Colorado. Mother had been an avid 4-H girl, traveling to Chicago in the 1950s as a member of a collegiate 4-H judging team. Was 4-H important to her? Let's just say she did not envision her daughters' lives without 4-H. I recall no discussion of whether or not I should join, nor did we discuss what projects I would take.

You won't be surprised to learned that my mom had signed me up for the 4-H sheep project. She helped me select the sheep I would train, groom, and show at the county fair—including Abe, a fuzzy-faced, mild Southdown lamb that I entered in the market-lamb class.

"There, you look so cute." I had fluffed up the thick woolly hair on his head and cheeks with a grooming tool (called a card) twenty minutes before I was scheduled to take Abe into his class.

"Card out his legs." Mom was holding Abe for me while I worked.

"I already did." Tired from a long day, my ambition had its limits. "Let's go, Abe." The announcer called, "Medium-weight Southdowns." That was our class.

The evening show-ring experience for a nine-year-old

nearing her bedtime was a blur. Focused on the judge and trying to remember the show-ring etiquette rules Mom had taught me, I did not realize until it was too late that Abe, who loved to nibble at my hair and clothing, had yanked the fabric ruffles off my pink Western shirt.

"No, no, Abe." I had no choice but to let the ruffles hang, as if the seamstress had neglected to stitch them onto the shirt. I was relieved when the judge placed the large class and gave his reasons.

The perky, teenage fair queen handed me a pink, fourth-place ribbon and chirped "Congratulations. Your lamb is really cute."

I hoped she, in her finery, didn't notice my dangling ruffle. Finally, contestants began to exit the show ring.

"You made it into the sale!" Mom beamed.

"I have to *sell* Abe?" Getting into the 4-H sale was a big deal. It meant generous buyers would pay inflated prices to buy the market animals raised by 4-H'ers.

I knew the animals we raised eventually went into either our own freezer or someone else's, but not until that moment did I fully realized this would be Abe's fate.

I cried on and off for two days. Preparing to bid farewell to Abe was not easy. Then the night of the annual county 4-H livestock sale arrived.

"Cheer up now, Marilyn." Mother recognized the tears ready to burst forth at any moment. "You're up next. Try to smile."

Somehow I was able to get Abe in and out of the show ring without crying, but as I returned my lamb to the pen, the dam broke. I sobbed.

"Wipe away your tears so you can tell Mr. Murphy thank-you for buying Abe. He paid nearly triple market price."

I hated the thought of squashing her enthusiasm.

"Thank you, Mr. Murphy, for buying … my lamb." Had I said "Abe," I would have again burst into tears. "I really appreciate it." I didn't feel at all thankful, though, and my blotchy eyes revealed the truth.

Abe wasn't the only lamb I showed and cried over.

The next year we moved to a larger farm a few miles north, and I joined the Galeton 4-H Club. Mother spotted a fast-growing, well-muscled lamb in our flock. We named the lamb Gomer, after the goofy television character, Gomer Pyle. I took Gomer to a show in May in a neighboring community. He had been born in February, so we were shocked when he weighed in at 109 pounds.

"Look, Mom, a blue ribbon." I waved my first-place ribbon as I left the show ring.

After the show, I saw my mother talking with the judge. Then she came over to me and said, "Marilyn, I know you like Gomer, and he has placed really well for you, but you are going to have to choose another lamb for county fair."

"Why?" After selling Abe the previous year at the county sale, I was resigned to the fate of Gomer, but this sounded like an exciting change of events. "Does that mean we keep him?"

"No, Marilyn, he's a wether (castrated male lamb). He won't make it to August." She hesitated. "Gomer will be over the hill, too large, by county fair. You'll have to choose a different lamb."

Choosing another lamb was not a problem. We had plenty. The problem—for me—was that Gomer went into our own freezer. I could not eat Gomer. It was purely psychological, but when the meat was served I choked on it. All I could think about was the living Gomer. I knew even then that I was being irrational. We raised meat sheep. They became meat to nourish people.

One day that summer my sisters and I had evening

softball practice, so our family ate supper early. What was on the menu? Lamb chops, of course. My sister, Shelly (who had the same psychological barrier as I had against eating Gomer) and I cut our lamb chops into bite-sized pieces. We put one or two bites into our mouths, and then when our parents weren't looking, we slipped the chunks of lamb chop into the Western riding boots we were wearing. When supper was over, our father asked if we didn't want to change into sneakers before we left for softball practice. We told him we did not, and left for the softball field. As soon as we arrived at the field, Shelly and I sprinted, as best we could in boots filled with chunks of lamb chop, to the outfield. We pulled off our boots and dumped the meat. We still laugh about that antic. (I can tell you, practicing softball in Western boots was not easy.)

Even to this day I wish we didn't have to kill animals to feed ourselves. I know this sounds strange coming from a sheep farmer. Our lambs are raised humanely and have good lives. I ensure they are killed in the most humane way possible. Scripture is very clear that eating flesh from animals is God's design for this world, albeit a fallen world.

Whether it is the slaughter of animals for meat, the passing of a person who has lived a long, good life, or the tragic death of a young person, death just seems wrong. According to King Solomon, among the wisest men who ever lived, God has set eternity in the human heart. Life on this earth is not all there is. I am not theologically trained enough to get into the discussion of the role of animals beyond this earth, but I do know that whether the life is animal or human, people have a sense that there is more than this earthly life. This sense of eternity may be the reason we prolong, through medical means, the lives of people and animals.

King Solomon opens the book of Ecclesiastes lamenting

that all human efforts are vain. By chapter 3 verse 11, he is declaring that God makes everything beautiful in its time. I used to think Ecclesiastes was contradictory and depressing. Now that I'm older and have lived through some of the pain of human life, I think I see what King Solomon is expressing. He is eloquently provoking us to think about our life on earth.

I'm a simple girl, so I say it this way: Life can have its joys and fulfillment. But it is also really hard, painful, and unfair. The good news is that life on earth is less than a breath when compared to eternity.

–Marilyn

To Ponder:

- What specific evidence do I see that God has set eternity in the human heart?
- How do I find the balance of being heavenly-minded yet working ardently for the Lord and enjoying the life he has given us on this earth?
- Am I glad or sad that life on earth is but a breath when compared to eternity?

To Pray:

Thank you, Good Shepherd, for putting eternity in our hearts. Let me find purpose and joy in my work here on this earth, but let me never be deceived into believing this is all there is. Let me marvel at the greatness of the God I serve. Thank you that your ways are higher than the ways of humankind and infinitely beyond anything we can fathom.

44
Bad Company Corrupts Good Character

Do not be misled: "Bad company corrupts good character." Come back to your senses as you ought, and stop sinning; for there are some who are ignorant of God—I say this to your shame.

–I Corinthians 15:33-34 (NIV)

Mother mixed the lamb's milk from powder, put nipples on the bottles, and instructed my two sisters and me to feed the bottle lambs. Marla, my youngest sister, reached into the bucket of 16-ounce Coke bottles, each filled with warm lamb's milk.

"I get to feed Pibb!"

"There are ten lambs to feed." I rolled my eyes at Marla and pulled the bucket away. "Wait until we get to the barn." I headed toward the barn, lugging the five-gallon bucket full of Coke bottles on my thigh.

Most of the bottle lambs were triplets whose mothers were unable to feed them enough milk but who still cared for and fed them what milk they could. A few of the lambs had lost their mothers to death or had been completely rejected by them. Pibb was one of the latter.

When Pibb was small, he would finish his bottle then follow us around the corral as we fed hay to the lambs and made sure all pens of sheep had fresh water. Bottle lambs, especially orphan lambs without a family, tend to bond with the humans who feed them. Pibb was an especially-persistent little guy, and when he was still quite young, we started letting him leave the corral with us. He'd follow us to the house and wait at the back door. He'd have come inside with us had we let him, but that is where Mother drew the line. No ambulatory lambs in the house!

After crossing the farmyard, we entered the sheep pen. True to her word, Marla grabbed a bottle and fed Pibb, who drank with gusto. When he finished, Marla got the bottle for the next lamb, but Pibb continued to wag his tail and butt at Marla's legs while she fed other lambs. Butting the ewe's udder is an instinctual behavior that lambs engage in when nursing from their mothers, because butting the ewe stimulates the production and release of her milk. Bottle lambs can very aggressively butt their human "mothers."

"I like you so much, Pibb," Marla said as she let the little lamb suck her fingers.

"We have other chores," I yelled over my shoulder, on my way to the haystack to throw hay to the ewes.

"I know." My little sister eventually tore herself away from Pibb, to help.

Chores completed, we exited the gate, Pibb in tow. He wagged his tail and butted Marla, and we had to squeeze ourselves through the back door, so the lamb wouldn't follow us inside the house.

When he was sure "his girls" would not be back outside until the next feeding, Pibb would hang out with our two farm dogs on—or curl up to nap on—the back porch steps in the afternoon sun.

On the weekends, my two sisters and I, still in elementary school, would entertain ourselves with whatever we found on the farm. (That was pre-video game days.) I didn't so much choose to play with Pibb as much as he chose us. He was always right there at our legs, looking for his bottle, wagging his tail, butting our legs. When we invited friends over to play, they were fascinated with Pibb and enjoyed playing with him. We put doll clothes on Pibb, fed him like a human baby cradled in our arms, strapped him into a saddle bag slung over a horse, and subjected the poor thing to just about anything else a bunch of redneck, little girls could dream up. But Pibb kept coming back. It was hard to walk from the house to the corral, because Pibb was there under foot.

During the long expanses of time when he had no humans to hang with or pester, Pibb bonded with the dogs and developed some of their behaviors. When someone drove into our yard, Pibb would follow the dogs as they barked at the "intruders." He would snuggle up with the dogs in their resting place at the back door and even followed them into the dog house when it snowed.

I never thought about how ridiculous Pibb's behavior was until one day a car pulled into our yard, and Pibb—and only Pibb—chased it. Apparently, it was a car the dogs recognized, so they did not go out to bark like they would have done with an unknown vehicle. However, new to guard duty, Pibb had missed this nuance. He was there, doing the dogs' job of protecting us from unknown peril. The driver was thoroughly amused by our "watch lamb." Eventually, Pibb, approaching 100 pounds, had to go back into the sheep corral. I'm sure in this day and age, had Pibb been a human, he would have required intensive identity counseling!

While Pibb's character was not corrupted by hanging out with our dogs, his behavior altered greatly. There are some dog behaviors, like biting or chewing things, which Pibb was biologically incapable of adopting. Nonetheless, the little guy did his best to mimic the behavior of the dogs. Pibb, our "watch lamb," made me think about the admonition from the Apostle Paul in I Corinthians 15:33, quoting Greek poet and dramatist Menander, who said, "Bad company corrupts good character."

Those of us who are parents have heard repeatedly from our older children that they can maintain their character even while hanging out with peers of much less than stellar character. We, along with the Apostle Paul, know this is highly unlikely. Most always, the individual of good character ends up mimicking the person of poor character. This is not to say we should not reach out to friends and acquaintances who are having moral struggles. We can and we should. But, we need to be very careful about how much time and where we spend time with anyone of questionable character, and be aware of who is influencing whom.

Menander also said, "The character of a man is known from his conversations." Perhaps an honest evaluation of my conversations when I am around a person of questionable character and when I am not is a good measuring stick for this person's influence over me.

–Marilyn

To Ponder:

- Am I keeping any "bad company?" If not human, is there a form of media or other habit or obsession that is my "bad company?"
- What measures might I take to ensure I am not being corrupted by bad company?

To Pray:

Protect me, Good Shepherd, from evil influences and wrong attitudes and habits. Help me to be discerning as I associate with people and participate in activities. Give me the courage to disassociate myself from close relationships with people of bad character and activities that hinder my relationship with you. Convict me of conversations that do not glorify you. Point out any influences that are causing me to engage in conversations that lead me away from the pursuit of godliness. Help me to reach out with your love to those who need you. And help me to find and nurture close friendships among fellow believers.

Marilyn's daughter Shannon provides "good company" to this bottle lamb, helping it get used to drinking from a modern bottle system—a bucket with nipples.

45
HOW'S YOUR HEART?

But the Lord said to Samuel, "Do not look at his appearance or at his physical stature, because I have refused him. For the Lord does not see as man sees; for man looks at the outward appearance, but the Lord looks at the heart." ... And Samuel said to Jesse, "Are all the young men here?" Then he said, "There remains yet the youngest, and there he is, keeping the sheep." And Samuel said to Jesse, "Send and bring him. For we will not sit down till he comes here." So he sent and brought him in. Now he was ruddy, with bright eyes, and good-looking. And the Lord said, "Arise, anoint him; for this is the one!"

–I Samuel 16:7, 11-12 (NKJV)

We were, and still are, simple folks. My father farmed hay, sugar beets, corn, wheat, and other crops. He also taught aviation at the community college. My mother took care of my two sisters and me, managed the house, and was the primary shepherd for our farm flock. We were not accustomed to knowing, much less entertaining, celebrities. So it was with a degree of nervousness that Mother informed us we would have Walter Younglund, state senator, at our home for dinner. He was an aviation student of my dad's.

"Dad and I expect you to use your very best manners. Be young ladies."

Mother inspected the table after my youngest sister Marla set it. Mom had separate plates for salad and dessert.

When Walt, as we were later instructed to call him, pulled into the driveway, we were surprised to see he drove an older car with plenty of dents and scratches.

Following introductions, Mom invited Senator Younglund to "Please, have a seat." Her shaking hand patted a chair at the end of the table opposite my dad's chair.

As the meal began, Marla announced, "Mom, I'm not hungry." She wasn't a fan of green salad.

Before Mom could respond, Walt pushed his plate toward Marla's. "I'll take your salad, young lady." He lifted Marla's salad plate and began to scrape the greens onto his own plate.

Mom looked like she was going to be sick. She reached for the serving bowl. "We have plenty of salad."

"No reason to waste this." Walt continued to push Marla's rejected salad onto his plate, trying to scrape off the last piece of lettuce. Then he exclaimed, "Oh, that must be your gum." He howled as if the punchline of a hilarious joke had just been delivered. "I'm color blind and didn't see it. Couldn't figure why it wouldn't come off your plate, young lady."

Mother turned pale.

Then we all burst out laughing.

This experience helps me identify with the Bible story in the Scripture above. I imagine the announcement of the impending visit to Jesse's home by Israel's prophet Samuel created every bit as much tension and excitement as did that first visit of Senator Younglund to our home.

Samuel had been instructed by God to go to Jesse and anoint one of his sons to be the next king of Israel. God was sad that Saul, Israel's first king had turned from him. Samuel also grieved Saul's sin, but was faithful to follow God's instructions, so he traveled to the home of Jesse.

Jesse was the grandson of Ruth, the Moabitess who left her homeland to accompany Naomi, the mother of her dead husband, back to the land of Israel, once the famine ended. Ruth defied the customs of the time when, instead of returning to her own people, she committed herself to Naomi, to the people of Israel, and to their God. Ruth later married Boaz, a wealthy landowner in whose fields she labored to collect grain left by the harvesters. If ever there was a case for a mother-in-law to proclaim that her son "could do better," this was it. Ruth was penniless, a widow, and a foreigner.

A look into Boaz's parentage reveals that his mother was Rahab, the harlot of Jericho, who saved the Hebrew spies from being discovered and killed. No doubt Rahab had taught Boaz compassion for the foreigner and to look beyond a person's outward appearance and social standing, to his or her heart. Boaz didn't hesitate in his love for Ruth, and he married her in honor.

Scripture indicates Jesse knew the purpose of Samuel's visit. Can you imagine that communication? "Jesse, God told me to anoint one of your sons—I don't know which one—to be the next king of Israel. How about I come over to your place next week, so we can get this done? One more thing, we need to keep this a secret; otherwise, Saul will kill us both."

Can't you just see Jesse lining up his sons? The proud papa presented seven sons to Samuel. In the I Samuel chapter 16 account, Samuel evaluated Eliab, the first son presented to him. Samuel commented, "Surely the Lord's anointed is before him," indicating that the prophet was impressed with the young man. God let Samuel know that he evaluates the heart, whereas Samuel saw only the young man's physical appearance. When God failed to give the nod to any of the seven sons Jesse had ready and waiting, Samuel asked Jesse whether he had another son.

"Oh, yes, there is another, an eighth son, but he is young," responded his father. "He is out keeping the sheep." That may sound picturesque, but I assure you when they fetched David, he was not as presentable as his brothers. Let's just say it: he probably stunk. Samuel notes that David was good looking with bright eyes and a ruddy complexion. I'm thinking the ruddy complexion may have been due to David's running in from the sheep field and having to be presented to the prophet without first bathing and changing his clothes.

This story of the shepherd-king's early life is precious to me; I love David's humble beginnings. He was the youngest in his family. Jesse failed to summon David when Samuel was on his way to choose a king from Jesse's sons, either because his father thought so little of him, or because David was such a good shepherd that he would be difficult to replace. Although the reason is more likely the former, I prefer to think it is the latter. Good shepherds *are* hard to replace!

God wasn't necessarily looking for a physically-impressive boy. He made it clear in this Scripture that the outward appearance was irrelevant. What God was concerned with when choosing a king of Israel, and what he is concerned with today in choosing those through whom he will do his work, is the heart. As we know from reading the rest of the story, David wasn't perfect. God chose to use David, even to put him in the genealogical line of Christ, because he sought after the Lord with all his heart. Not only had David grown physically strong and learned to be a leader and a warrior as he tended sheep, he had learned to seek God. God called David a "man after my own heart."

Don't let the evil one ever tell you that you are not good enough or talented enough, that you don't have enough spiritual insight, or that your parentage is inadequate to serve Christ. The Good Shepherd often chooses the weak things of this world to demonstrate his strength.

–Marilyn

TO PONDER:

• Have I believed any of the lies Satan has whispered to me to discredit my ability to serve? If it is a past sin for which I have confessed and repented, or a circumstance beyond my control, I can put it behind me.

• Can I truly accept that God wants to use me as I am?

• Am I devoting time to making and keeping my heart tender toward the things of God?

TO PRAY:

Mighty Shepherd, my failures reinforce my desperate need of you. But I look away now from myself and my failures, to you. Forgive me for listening to Satan's condemnation of me for my past. Correct the lies that these accusations have planted in my heart and mind. Instead, I want to live in the truth of who I am in you. Help me to rest in the arms of my Shepherd. Make my heart tender toward you and what is important to you. Though I am weak, make me strong in your might. Thank you for the wonder and beauty of this world you have created. I want to live every day in the joy of your presence. I offer myself and my talents to be used in your kingdom any way you choose.

"Gentle as a lamb"

Glossary

4-H– a youth organization; H's stand for Head, Hands, Health, Heart
banding– applying special small, doughnut-shaped bands to tails and testicles, causing them to detach from the body
bloat– a disease caused by ingesting, especially, legumes; can also be caused by excess fermentation of grain intake; often fatal if left untreated; the stomach fills with so much gas that it presses on the diaphragm and causes suffocation
branding– for identifying individuals; sheep are marked with a special wool-paint which is applied with numbered tools
bottle lamb– lamb which must receive its milk from a bottle
carding– combing the fleece with a special hand-held tool
castrating– act of removing the testicles from a male lamb
corral– enclosure for animals; can vary in size
cud– a ball of partly digested food which the sheep must burp up and further chew before swallowing again
docking– procedure to shorten the tail
ear tag– a plastic or metal tag with an identification number or name on it, applied to the ear with a special hand-held tool
enterotoxemia– a bacterial infection which grows rapidly in the digestive system, producing a toxin which causes, usually, death
ewe– female sheep
F.F.A.– Future Farmers of America; a youth organization
flock, herd– a group of sheep
jug– small pen to contain a new sheep mother and her baby/babies
lambing– act of a sheep giving birth
lambing barn– special shelter for ewes getting ready to give (or that already have given) birth
pull a lamb– assist a sheep in delivering her baby/babies
ram– an un-neutered male sheep
rendering truck– truck which hauls away dead animals
ruminants– cud-chewing animals which do best eating some form of the grass family
shearing– the act of removing a sheep's wool, usually with hand-held clippers or an electric tool
Southdown– short, blocky-statured sheep with light tan faces and legs, primarily raised for meat
Suffolk– large meat-breed sheep with black faces and legs
wether– neutered male sheep

Index of Scriptures

About the Authors

Marilyn Bay Wentz graduated with a BA in Journalism and a minor in Spanish from the University of Northern Colorado. She edits two national agriculture publications, *Bison World* and *Open Pastures*. Prior to settling down in her native Colorado, she was general manager of the Taiwan public relations branch of Saatchi and Saatchi Advertising, then the world's largest advertising agency, and also spent six months in rural Costa Rica. She is fluent in Spanish and speaks conversational Mandarin Chinese. She now operates Prairie Natural Lamb. She also enjoys training horses, is a certified Colorado 4-H horse show judge, and is an AWANA leader. Marilyn has authored a novel, *Prairie Grace* (Koehler). She enjoys her two daughters—Kelly, who is grown and married, and Shannon, who is in high school.

Find Marilyn online at her website: www.MarilynBayWentz.com/. Follow her on Facebook at Marilyn Bay Wentz.

Mildred Nelson Bay (Millie) is Marilyn's mother. She has lived in Colorado all her life except for two years in Fairbanks, Alaska. Millie has served as an AWANA leader, Sunday School teacher, member of Gideons International, and a 4-H leader. Millie has raised sheep for forty years, including lambing-out as many as 100 ewes per year. As a writer, she has had numerous articles published in local newspapers and several in the *State Gideon Lamp*. Millie and her husband, Marvin, have three grown daughters and ten grandchildren.

Learn more about this and other Cladach titles
and their authors at
www.CLADACH.com.